THE MEN'S ADVENTURE LIBRARY

EXOTIC

Adventures of ROBERT SILVERBERG

EDITORS — Robert Deis and Wyatt Doyle   DESIGNED BY — Wyatt Doyle

TABLE OF CONTENTS

EXOTIC ADVENTURES OF ROBERT SILVERBERG, ISBN 978-1-943444-22-9 A New Texture book for The Men's Adventure Library, © 2021 Subtropic Productions LLC. Stories © 1957, 1985 by Agberg, Ltd., reprinted by permission. Cover portrait by Jimmy Angelina; original cover painting by Rafael DeSoto. Special thanks to Matthias Belz. Materials courtesy The Robert Deis Archive. Printed in the USA.

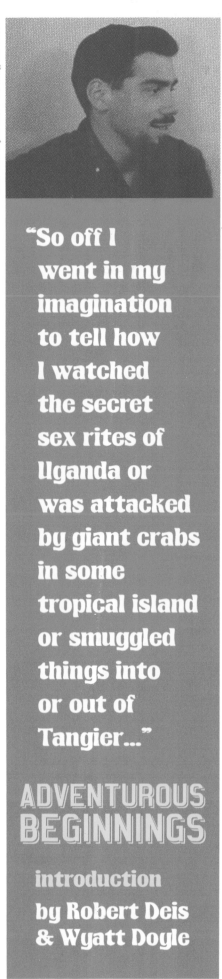

"So off I went in my imagination to tell how I watched the secret sex rites of Uganda or was attacked by giant crabs in some tropical island or smuggled things into or out of Tangier..."

ADVENTUROUS BEGINNINGS

introduction by Robert Deis & Wyatt Doyle

"I have to confess, right up front here, that you will not find a great deal in the way of poetic vision in these stories, or singing prose, or deep insight into character. Nor are these stories that will tell you much that is new to you about the human condition. These are stories in what is now pretty much a lost tradition...the simple and unselfconsciously fast-paced adventure story of the pulp-magazine era. They are stories from the dawn of my career...and are straightforward tales of action, in the main, that were written partly for fun and partly for money." [1]

ROBERT Silverberg is renowned as one of the world's greatest authors of science fiction stories and novels, and is beloved by millions of readers worldwide for his work in that genre. He has received virtually all of the top honors given to writers in the realm of speculative fiction, including multiple Hugo Awards and Nebula Awards and induction into the Science Fiction and Fantasy Hall of Fame.

However, Silverberg's long career as a writer includes many detours that are less well known. And though in the quote above he was speaking of his early SF work, the same could be said of a set of stories penned during one of those detours, writing under a long list of pseudonyms in 1958 and 1959 for *Exotic Adventures*, a short-lived men's adventure magazine. And, though those tales are not science fiction, most could be called fantasy—or, more specifically, men's action/adventure fantasy.

That's essentially what most fiction stories in the men's adventure magazines, or MAMs, published in the 1950s, 1960s, and 1970s were: Pulpy tales involving danger, excitement, sexy women, and violence.

They are actually not far removed from the type of stories Silverberg wrote earlier in his career for magazines in the science fiction and fantasy subgenre of the larger genre of pulp fiction, the all-fiction magazines with fantastic painted cover art that

were hugely popular during the first half of the 20th century.

Silverberg began writing science fiction stories in 1954, when he was a sophomore at Columbia College in New York City. He made a few sales and even managed to land a well-connected agent, Scott Meredith, whose literary agency represented and boosted the careers of scores of top writers.

Meredith also repped two science fiction writers who happened to live in the same building as Silverberg and became his close friends. One was Harlan Ellison, the other was Randall Garrett.

In 1955, Garrett not only helped Silverberg get stories placed in various SF mags, he also formed a writing partnership with him. Together, in the late '50s they co-wrote dozens of stories under the pseudonym *Robert Randall* and essentially became the staff writers for several science fiction magazines published by William L. Hamling via his Greenleaf publishing company, including *Imagination*, *Imaginative Tales*, and *Fantastic Adventures*.

By 1958, Silverberg's career as a science fiction writer was booming—and lucrative. However, the market for science fiction magazines was drying up: "A dozen or so magazines for which I had been writing regularly ceased publication overnight; and as for the tiny market for SF novels (two paperback houses and one hardcover) it suddenly became so tight that unless you were one of the first-magnitude stars like Robert Heinlein or Isaac Asimov you were out of luck." [2]

Silverberg began writing for growing markets in newer genres, including crime digest magazines like *Trapped*, *Guilty*, and *Manhunt*, MAMs such as *Male*, *For Men Only*, *Men*, *Man's Magazine*, *Stag*, and *True Men Stories*, and "bachelor magazines" inspired by the success of *Playboy*, such as *Rogue* and *Adam*.

Silverberg "only occasionally" read magazines in these new genres. "I was primarily a science-fiction writer and that was the field I kept up with." But he was a professional storyteller, limited only by his ambition and imagination—and Silverberg had both in ample supply. Before long, he had published dozens of stories in the crime digest magazines, and Meredith started brokering his stories to MAMs.

Monty Howard had been an associate editor for two of Hamling's SF magazines, and by late 1957, he "was running a couple of low-rent *Playboy* imitators called *Venus* and *Mermaid*, and was starting one of those men's adventure mags, to be called *Exotic Adventures*. He needed a lot of copy, fast. I sold Monty a few short stories for the fiction magazines, and then he asked me to do some tales of, well, exotic adventure for *Exotic Adventures*."

Despite its lack of exotic setting, Silverberg saw his sexy college yarn "Campus Hellcat" published in the first issue. (It was later reprinted in—and used as the title for—a 1960 collection of Silverberg's racy stories.)

"He liked it so much that he asked for another, and another, and before long I was writing practically the whole magazine."

He had no stories in the second issue, then three in the third. Silverberg could crank out all kinds of "exotic adventure" style stories quickly and reliably. Thus, he ended up writing most of the stories published in the final three issues, between black-and-white photo spreads featuring near-nude women.

"They had a formula: protagonist gets in trouble in some far-off part of the world, preferably with some sexual entanglement—and I stayed with it."

Exotic Adventures was a sort of hybrid between a MAM and a bachelor magazine. It didn't last long. Four issues were published in 1958, and two in 1959.

"Low-rent *Playboy* imitators" *Mermaid* and *Venus* enjoyed equally brief lifespans. They were published by Garden of Eve Publications, while *Exotic Adventures* was published by Gladiator Publications. Both companies had the same address: 222 West 33rd Street, New York. The name Monty Howard does not appear on any of their mastheads. Indeed, the names of the magazines' editorial staff don't seem to appear anywhere else *except* on the mastheads of those three short-lived magazines, suggesting that they may have been pseudonyms to keep the real names of the staff and publishers from being known to potential censors—or creditors.

There was a lot of entrepreneurial publishing in those years, and the evidence suggests *Exotic Adventures* was such an effort—perhaps as something of an experiment, or test flight.

Whatever the truth behind Gladiator Publications, they were not a major MAM publisher—nor a major publisher, period. *Exotic Adventures* was not a top-tier MAM. Nor was it representative of the enduring successes in the field. It differs from more fondly remembered titles in several key aspects, starting with one of MAMs' most important elements: the artwork. There are few artists of note in its pages, and despite some appealing line art, several interior spreads look rushed and cheap. Arresting illustration art is a MAM hallmark, and *Exotic Adventures* simply didn't deliver quality work consistently—something taken for granted in every issue of higher-tier MAMs. A MAM's fortunes were partly dependent on its artwork, and there *Exotic Adventures* came up short.

Yet it *is* representative of another aspect of MAM publishing: the industry's minnows and pilot fish, small fry eager to capitalize on a popular and profitable concept. After all, this was a field where profitable ideas were swiped and copied as a matter of course, and there was no shortage of quick-buck efforts riding the trend. All told, there were about 160 MAM titles offered by multiple publishers over three decades. For every quality, standard-bearing MAM

Advertisement for MERMAID from EXOTIC ADVENTURES Vol. 1, No. 2 (1958)

3

MAN'S MAGAZINE
September 1965

In the frankest, most vivid conversations ever recorded, a group of women bare their most secret sexual feelings to a top American doctor.

—Stag, March 1970

from the likes of Magazine Management Company, there were smaller, short-lived mags like *Exotic Adventures* drafting behind the popularity of the more professionally produced titles, chasing a piece of the action. You can't have a proper gold rush without prospectors and opportunists, and the cheap, the rushed, and the scrappy are just as integral a part of the MAM era and its history as the top-tier titles. What's more, it's only cheap and scrappy operations like *Exotic Adventures* that would have even considered relying on a single writer working under a dozen pseudonyms for nearly its entire table of contents.

And that's the most obvious appeal of *Exotic Adventures*' six-issue run: The opportunity to read Robert Silverberg writing in men's adventure mode, and vicariously thrilling to the

unique circumstances of these stories' creation. The idea of Silverberg, the consummate young pro, nimbly genre-hopping, hammering out entire issues of pulp fiction at a breakneck pace, a John Henry at the typewriter, is irresistible, and the stuff of legend for writers born too late to work for MAMs. Silverberg's prolific early career is both testament to the writer's mastery of his craft and a reminder of the days—now long past—when a hungry wordsmith with enough discipline and talent could build his portfolio (and bank balance) penning wild tales of adventure and sex, stories that sold and saw print almost as quickly as they could be set down on paper.

Inevitably, aspects of all vintage adventure fiction age poorly, with elements that rankle contemporary sensibilities.

But as reflections of their time, place, and intended readership, it should come as no surprise when such stories are out of step with contemporary sensibilities.

MAM readers of that era tended to be working class, and a sizable number of them veterans of WWII and Korea. Many who returned had developed fresh interest and curiosity about the places their service took them and the cultures they encountered. It's a fascination that had been in the air for some decades, notably reflected in the work of fine artists like Gauguin and novels and stories by Melville, Conrad, and Robert Louis Stevenson, among others. But this postwar surge of interest in exotica proved particularly infectious, and it was a time when foreign places and cultures, particularly those perceived as romantic and mysterious, tended to inspire more fascination than suspicion or hostility. Before long, those fascinations permeated the larger culture, in aspects ranging from cuisine to fashion to decor and architecture, and they informed popular diversions from music and dance to movies to fiction—MAM fiction especially. While these expressions were generally enthusiastic, they were not necessarily nuanced or authentic, and some are now seen as unflattering burlesques of the cultures they appeared to celebrate.

Sorting out genuine interest and curiosity from exploitation has been a source of near-constant discussion in the decades since, and it is far too complex a debate to do justice here. Silverberg's position on his vintage fiction is clear: "I was writing those stories more than sixty years ago for the readers of that era and in the manner of that era. Modern political correctness can't be applied retroactively to things written so long ago."

A CASE could be made that Silverberg's *Exotic Adventures* stories paved the way for the next and most lucrative phase of his early career—as one of America's most prolific writers of sex novels.

Many *Exotic Adventures* stories have sex scenes, but none are particularly graphic. "Everything was done by euphemism and metaphor. No explicit anatomical descriptions were allowed, no naughty words. About as far as you could go was a phrase like *'they were lying together, and he felt the urgent thrust of her body against him, and his aroused maleness was penetrating her, and he felt the warm soft moist clasping and the tightening...'"* [2]

Sex scenes in Silverberg's *Exotic Adventures* work are generally brief, and usually aren't the stories' focus. But they do seem infused with more sexual heat than fiction published in more mainstream MAMs in the late '50s. It would be the 1960s before most MAMs featured stories with comparable "euphemism and metaphor"

sex scenes.

By then, MAMs were publishing a different type of Silverberg sex story: "sexology" articles, penned as *L.T. Woodward, M.D.*

William Hamling, who played a key role in Silverberg's initial success as a writer of science fiction, went on to play a key role in Silverberg's success as a writer of sex novels and sexology books and articles.

In 1959, Hamling started publishing soft-porn paperback novels via Greenleaf and its various subsidiaries, such as Nightstand Books, Midnight Reader, and Regency Books.

Scott Meredith recruited many of the writers he'd represented to write sex novels for Hamling. Soon, Meredith was the largest supplier of porn manuscripts in the country. Among the writers he tapped to write soft porn for Hamling under pseudonyms were Robert Bloch, Philip José Farmer, B. Traven, and Kurt Vonnegut.

Silverberg was only 24 years old when he began writing sex novels for Hamling, and his output in that field is staggering. Between 1959 and 1964, he wrote 150 soft porn novels, all published under pseudonyms, most frequently *Don Elliott*.

Though he couldn't get and didn't want any public notoriety for that work at the time, he enjoyed writing them—and it paid extremely well by most writers' standards. Silverberg started out being paid about $600 per book, with bonuses for high production. He was soon cranking out an average of two sex novels per month and making an average of $1,000 per week—the equivalent of over $400,000 per year in today's dollars.

In the 1960s, Silverberg capitalized on the craze for "sexology" books—books that provided overviews or exposés of sexual topics. These books include titillating descriptions and details about the sex lives of hetero-, homo-, and bisexual men and women. But they have a veneer of respectability and believability that starts with the titles given to the pseudonymous

authors. Most alleged to be written by doctors, professors, or some other type of seemingly reliable expert.

For his sexology books, Silverberg used his *L.T. Woodward, M.D.* pseudonym. His fellow Meredith agency writer Lawrence Block also penned a number of sexology books under the name *Dr. Benjamin Morse.*

Scott Meredith sold excerpts from Silverberg's and Block's sexology books for publication as articles in various MAMs. Thus, Silverberg's non-fiction books as Woodward, such as *1001 Answers to Vital Sex Questions* (1962), *Virgin Wives* (1962), *Twilight Women* (1963), *I Am a Nymphomaniac* (1965), and *Sophisticated Sex Techniques in Marriage* (1967) would be excerpted as MAM articles under the Woodward byline, like "The Male Nymphomaniac" (*Man's Magazine*, December 1963), "Sex Lives of Nurses" (*Man's Magazine*, November 1966), "Sex Lives of Models" (*Man's Magazine*, February 1966) and "Sex in the Balcony" (*Guy*, 1968 Annual). Articles adapted from L.T. Woodward sexology texts are the most common stories by him in the major MAMs.

The stories he wrote for *Exotic Adventures* in 1958 and 1959 comprise the majority of Silverberg's MAM fiction. (That he didn't write more after that suggests how busy he became writing sex novels after 1959.) But his adventure fiction does appear in another MAM/bachelor hybrid, *Sir!* Its July 1959 issue features a grim Cold War story written as *Mark Ryan*, titled "The Women's Slave Barracks." And an exotic adventure story from *Sir!*'s November 1959 issue is reprinted in the Men's Adventure Library anthology *Weasels Ripped My Flesh!* Credited to his pseudonym *David Challon*, it's titled "Mattern's 50 Days as an Amazon Love Slave."

"Absolutely autobiographical," says Silverberg. ●

1 "Introduction," *In the Beginning: Tales from the Pulp Era* (Subterranean Press, 2006)

2 "My Life as a Pornographer," *Sin-A-Rama* (Feral House, 2005, 2016)

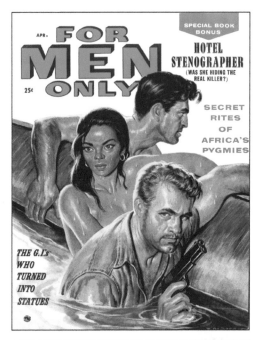

FOR MEN ONLY
April 1957

ACTION FOR MEN
March 1960

MAN'S PERIL
March 1964

MAM publishers often reused cover paintings for more than one issue of their own magazines, and sometimes as interior illustrations. Occasionally they appropriated artwork originally commissioned and utilized by other publishers.

The painting on the cover of the first issue of *Exotic Adventures* in 1958 is a version of artwork originally created for the cover of *For Men Only*, April 1957 by Rafael DeSoto (1904-1992). The original piece included a second man on the other side of the canoe.

For Men Only was one of the popular, long-running "Diamond" line of MAMs published by subsidiaries of Magazine Management Company, founded by Martin Goodman, who also created Marvel Comics. Magazine Management reused DeSoto's painting on the cover of the March 1960 issue of another long-running Diamond MAM, *Action for Men*, though the image was reversed on that cover.

The painting's next (likely unauthorized) use was by the short-lived, low-budget company Gladiator Publications, Inc., for the first issue of *Exotic Adventures*. The second man was painted out.

That altered version was later reused on the cover of *Man's Peril*, March 1964, published by Periodical Publishers, a company a slight step above Gladiator.

Interestingly, only the last of the four magazines that feature DeSoto's painting actually runs a story that corresponds with the image. In *Man's Peril*, March 1964, "I Saved the Love Goddess from the Volcano Horror" includes a scene in which a pistol-packing American and a Javanese native girl make an escape by canoe.

(Atypically, that story's *interior* illustration by Norm Eastman appeared on the cover of the next issue of *Man's Peril* (May 1964), paired with a story set in Mexico, "We Found the City of Branded Virgins." It's a rare example of a cover painting that originated as an interior illustration, rather than the more common reuse of cover art as interior pieces. The female model for the virgins was one of Eastman's favorites: Eva Lynd, the actress, model, and pinup profiled in The Men's Adventure Library's *Eva: Men's Adventure Supermodel*.)

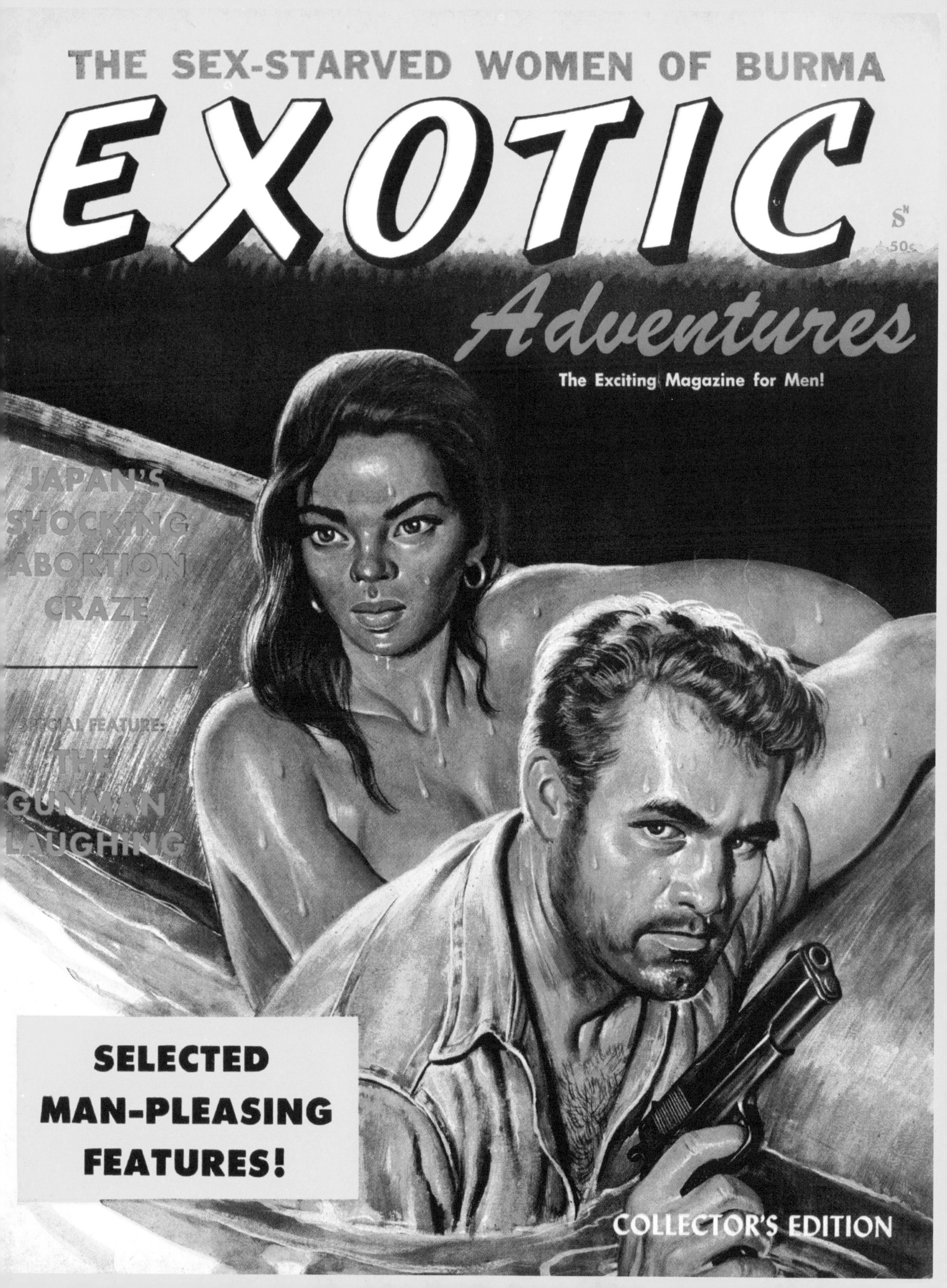

THE SEX-STARVED WOMEN OF BURMA

EXOTIC

S^A^N

50¢

Adventures

The Exciting Magazine for Men!

JAPAN'S
SHOCKING
ABORTION
CRAZE

SPECIAL FEATURE:
THE
GUNMAN
LAUGHING

**SELECTED
MAN-PLEASING
FEATURES!**

COLLECTOR'S EDITION

We parked the car and before I knew what was happening, she threw her arms around me and started fumbling with my belt buckle.

CAMPUS HELLCAT

There's one like her on every campus in the country. They'll do anything, anywhere, anytime. It's a great way to get an education.

SHE was wearing an extra-tight beige sweater, and when she leaned back to see what the Geology prof was drawing on the blackboard the view made me dizzy. I've got a good imagination. I was picturing the jutting breasts that made the sweater look that way.

I had never so much as spoken to the girl, but since the beginning of the semester I had filled up dull hours in class by refining my mental image of those breasts. I was sure the image was just about perfect—and *oh, my*! It was almost as if she were sitting nude in the classroom and only my eyes could see her.

As she leaned back the eye in my mind saw twin mounds of white flesh, soft and yet firm, tipped with hardening dots of pink. They rose and fell gently with each breath; my own breathing wasn't quite as regular.

"Geologically speaking, mountain formations of this type are known as—"

The acid rasp of Professor Thayer's voice yanked me out of Elysium. Reluctantly I glanced at the board and began to copy his sketch: two humped, rounded hills with a stream winding through them. My pencil raced over the paper. I sketched the hills, the stream ... added upthrust nipples, beckoning hips, silk-smooth thighs ...

I looked at what I had drawn and my hands started to quiver. *Dammit,*

(Continued on next page)

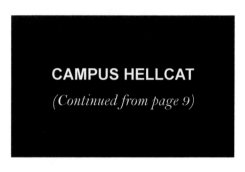

they shouldn't let girls into men's classes, I thought angrily. *I was an A student till she decided to take Geology.*

I couldn't follow the lecture. I couldn't take notes. I couldn't do anything but sit there in a sick sweat of desire, longing to run down the aisle, rip away her clothing, and throw myself on her. To Hell with Geology! There were better things in life!

Very carefully I saw to it that I was about a yard behind her as we left the lecture hall. We walked down the corridor that way—it was lunchtime—and now my imagination had a new field to play, as I contemplated the pair of trim buttocks just before me. They were sheathed in the sort of shapeless skirt college girls think is classy, but the impatient eye of my mind stripped it away and dreamily lay bare those pink curves.

"Pardon me," I said, suddenly stepping forward. "You're Miss Hallock, aren't you?"

She giggled. "Hello. I know you. You're in my Geology class. I think I saw you in the back row."

"That's right. Pretty tough course, isn't it?"

"It's a corker," she said. "I'm darned if I can keep up with all that dull stuff. Ignaceous and sentimental and—"

"No, no! *Igneous. Sedimentary.*"

She glanced at me slyly as we reached the steps of Avery Hall. "You sound like you know your stuff."

"A little," I admitted. "But I had a head start. I was always interested in Geology, even when I was a kid." *(Yeah,* I thought. *Especially in a pair of rocks like those.)*

"I've been having a lot of trouble," she said. "I'm beginning to think girls shouldn't take the course." She sighed,

and her sweater went taut. I stared deliriously, then managed to yank my eyes away before she noticed. *Easy, now,* I warned myself. One more display like that and I was likely to have at her right here in the Quadrangle. It would make wonderful headlines for the campus paper the next day ... but I wasn't interested in that sort of publicity.

Moistening my lips nervously, I said, "Don't give up. The Midterm Exam's getting close—but maybe you could find someone who'll give you some coaching. It's really not a hard subject once you overcome your natural repugnance for it."

"I think you're right," she said. "I think it can be a lot of fun if it's done the right way." For a moment I thought she was referring to something else, but then she added, "That's why I took the course."

"Sure. Say—the Midterm's next Thursday. How about you and me—ah—studying together? I'd be happy to help you out."

She turned, breasts heaving, eyes wide. "Oh, *would* you?" she asked, delighted, and I knew I had it made.

"Here's my place," I said tensely. She ducked around under my arm and stepped in.

"It's lovely. I like it." A little giggle. "Somehow I like *everything* today."

"Even Geology?"

"Even Geology."

I was living in a one-room hotel flat a couple of blocks from the College, sharing it with another undergrad named Phil Thomas. Phil was a tall, slick, wolfish sort who seemed to have a full-time haymaking proposition going with some girl of other pretty steadily. I wasn't quite so lucky—but I was planning to make up for lost time now, and I knew Phil would go purple with jealousy when he saw the sort of fullbosomed wench *I* brought home to keep me warm. He dated a series of bedraggled bags who were perfectly happy to yield their alabaster bodies in return for the glorious thrill of having slept with Phil Thomas—

or anyone. But I had something here that was something special, a seductive little lassie with bedroom eyes and—I hoped—bedroom thighs.

As I closed the door I yanked down the little flag outside, as a signal in case Phil came home unexpectedly. My classes were mostly in the morning and his in the afternoon, but we didn't want each other blundering in while one of us was in the process of making some silly co-ed come across.

I dumped my books on my bed, which was the lower berth in a double-decker, and put up a pot of coffee. Diana—that was her name, goddess of virginity, and I sure hoped that wasn't a bad omen—hung up her jacket and plunked herself down while I busied myself at the stove.

"There's a note on the bed, Steve," she said.

"Let me see."

I took it away before she had unfolded it, and read it. It was from Phil. It said, "Dear Nothing. I'm going home to visit my benighted parents this evening, and so the shack is all yours for the night. Pity you broke off with that freshman slut; it's a shame to waste all that good privacy. Phil."

"Anything important?"

"It's from my roommate. He's not coming home tonight."

"Oh?"

"I mean—he's going to visit his folks." Chuckling hollowly, I added, "That sort of means I'm in for a lonely night. Phil and I usually stay up having a bull session till three or so before we sack out."

"That the best thing you can do at night?" she asked, her voice suddenly throaty.

I started to tingle. I suddenly realized I'd grabbed hold of a livewire powerhouse, if that tone in her voice meant anything. *Poor Phil,* I thought pityingly. *He decided not to take Geology. The good-looking bastard doesn't know what he missed out on—yet.*

We started to study, sitting primly side-by-side on my lumpy mattress. I don't think my mind has ever been

8 MM MOVIES
ONLY 80¢ EACH

Why pay $2.00 or more for 50-ft. adult movies when you can get the very best for only 80c?

5 FILMS for $4.00
OR 12 FOR ONLY $9.00 !

YOU DON'T NEED A PROJECTOR

You don't need an expensive projector to view 50 ft 8mm movies. Order the new 8mm Movie Viewer and see sparkling life-life 50 ft. films in fast or slow motion.

$5.95 POSTPAID

100 ft. 8mm MOVIES
$1.60 EACH
5 for only $8.00

200 ft. 8mm MOVIES
$3.20 EACH
5 for only $16.00

11

less on Geology than it was at that moment.

But I stuck grimly to the task of instructing her. I led her through the mysteries of igneous, sedimentary, and metamorphic, taught her the difference between basalt and rock salt, explained all about the mesozoic and the protozoic. I guess I must have given her as much garbled information as the real poop, but I couldn't help that. My endocrine system was all out of kilter; hormones were flooding all over the place, and my body was tense with desire. We both knew what we had come up here for—and it wasn't to talk about fossils.

Only we had to keep up the pretense. That's the way life works, I had discovered. You don't take off the masks too soon.

So along about two in the afternoon, after an hour of good hard serious studying, I let myself edge closer to her on the bed. She was really wrapped up in the massively dull textbook, and I slid my hand up her bare, tender arm till it reached the smoothness of that beige sweater.

Then suddenly she wriggled and her breast cupped itself in my palm. Some handful. Through the sweater, through the bra, I could feel the stony hardness of the desire-swollen nipple. Gently, I tightened my grip, and the way her breathing changed I knew things were happening to her.

But we kept up the pretense. She didn't look up, but kept her nose in that book. Her heart was doing sixty, I could feel—and I wasn't too cool myself.

About two more minutes went by, seeming like an hour, and then she tucked her legs up underneath herself. Her skirt slid up above her knee. Thoughtfully I touched her calf, still fondling her breast with my other hand. Then, encountering no resistance, I let my hand upward, along her knee, into the cool hollow behind her knee, then suddenly between her warm, firm thighs—

The textbooks went thudding to the floor. She left hers there. I left mine

there. I thought of those poor saps in my Geology class, and wondered why *I* was the lucky one who was reaping this particular harvest.

A second later I stopped bothering to wonder. She was all over me, her warm body squirming against mine, her full, heavy breasts grinding into mine I heard her husky voice say, "Geology can wait, Steve."

"It sure can."

I peeled away her sweater, revealing a bra straining to contain the warm flesh inside it. I fumbled with the snaps, but they were too tight; impatiently, she ripped the flimsy thing off. Her breasts, free, jounced out.

They made the feeble doodlings of my imagination look scrawny. They were magnificent milk-white globes, each tipped with a smooth circlet of red-brown from which rose the tiny hard hill of a nipple. Full, rounded, her breasts rose and fell; she gasped with desperate urgency, making little harsh animal-noises. Her hands dropped to my belt.

With what seemed like terrible slowness we undressed each other. When she was completely naked, I leaned back; the scientist in me, I guess, wanted to observe the phenomenon in all its completeness. It was worth observing. She had a fantastic woman's body.

Broad shoulders and a proud throat, curving into those inviting breasts; a flat belly, indented faintly with the red line her filmy panties had left; long, slim, totally delightful legs below enticingly-swelling hips.

Hungrily, I buried my face in her breasts as I had so many times in my dreams. I felt the pulsing of her heart behind the soft warmness of the breasts thrust against me.

I caught a glimpse of her eyes, half-closed, mere slits smoky with desire. Our clothing mingled in a tangled heap on the floor, down there with the confusion of rapidly discarded notebooks and textbooks. Geology, college itself all seemed a pale dream from which we had suddenly awakened—

Awakened into *this*. Awakened

into this panting, frantic, love-hungry desperate world of sweat-slippery bodies. We clung to each other.

This was real. This was *it!*

Her teeth nipped my shoulder; my hands cupped her hot breasts, my thighs ground against her thighs.

Our bodies locked in a passionate embrace.

For a moment I thought desire would carry me away instantly. Deliberately I let ugly words run through my mind: *igneous, sedimentary, metamorphic, plateau, brachiopod,* distracting me from the call of pleasure while she writhed in fantastic contortions beneath me.

Her breath came harder, in short chunky bursts. She clung to me, her nails digging into my arms and shoulders, and I heard her panting, murmuring incoherent sounds of love.

Suddenly her burning body went taut, her eyes closed tight. Holding to each other, we shuddered out our ecstasy, and floated away together on a riptide of pleasure.

Later, after a balmy afternoon in which we lay together, body pressed against perspiring body, letting the mundane universe slowly ebb back into existence around us, we reluctantly returned to our studies. My mind was cloaked in a pleasant haze; I relived over and again the thunderous moment of climax. We were dressed again— but never hence would I need to use my imagination to conjure up what lay beneath the tight beige sweater and the shapeless skirt.

I knew.

I took her to dinner at a campus eatery; we stopped off at the Den for some dancing afterward. We went through the meaningless motions of a couple of foxtrots clasped together, smiling into each other's eyes as if to show the other couples in the Den that we shared something special, unique.

When I dropped her off at the gate to her dorms, she kissed me tenderly. "It's been a wonderful day, Steve … and I *know* I'll do marvelously well on that old Geo exam now."

"Of course you will, kitten."

I turned away, walking at least six feet in the air. I didn't mind spending the rest of the night alone now.

Phil returned from his safari homeward the next day, and I told him all about it—vividly. His eyes lit up with frank envy, and sudden pride surged in me. For all his procession of willing broads, I had topped him in spades.

"I think I'm in love," I said. "Maybe I'll even get married, Phil. This kid's really got it—and she's saving it all for me!"

"Yeah, yeah," he jeered. "If she'll do it for you, she'll do it for anyone. That's the way the world works, kid."

But I wasn't having any of his two-bit cynicism. He was just jealous; I knew that. I couldn't wait till tomorrow afternoon, when I was going to see Diane again.

Only she wasn't in the Quad at the time she was supposed to be. Chilled. I remembered Phil's acid words, then shook my head. It couldn't be. I had seen the love smoking in her eyes. Real love, not just bed-love.

But after waiting an hour or so in the nippy late-October air, I shrugged my shoulders and started to my flat, feeling as if the world had ended. It hadn't—yet.

I turned the key in the door and went in.

They were on my bed—*my* bed, because they hadn't had time to climb to the upper. Phil was wearing nothing but a pair of undarned socks. He was stretched out flat on his face snoozing the snooze of the man who's been well laid, and, sitting up in the bed, clutching her knees to her lush breasts in a halfhearted attempt to hide her nakedness—

Diane.

My first reaction was one of anger and embarrassment; why the hell hadn't Phil tripped the signal if he was going to be fooling around in our room?

Then my numbed mind caught on. "Hello," I said icily.

"Hello," Diane stammered, looking very nude and very guilty. She sprang from the bed and dashed across the

floor into the adjoining john; I caught a brief glimpse of bobbing breasts, flashing thighs, ripe buttocks. The door slammed. Phil woke, rolled over, and looked up at me.

"Guess I forgot the signal," he said, grinning affably. "Sorry, old man."

Sorry! Here he was in bed with my girl and all he could think of was to apologize about not pulling down the signal? My tongue was a cold lump in my throat.

"That girl," I said, gesturing toward the john. "That girl—"

"Lovely chick, isn't she?" He beamed proudly. "Name's Diane. She's in my Astronomy class. I brought her up here little while ago to coach her for the Midterm—and the damndest thing happened!"

The end

While Silverberg does not appear in the second issue of *Exotic Adventures*, it includes "The Island of Tyooah," an early story by writer and iconoclast Harlan Ellison, as well as "The Bewitched King" by George H. Smith, an author of science fiction and softcore adult novels and stories under various pseudonyms. The cover painting by Hugh Hirtle is also noteworthy for clearly using Bettie Page as the model for the damsel in distress.

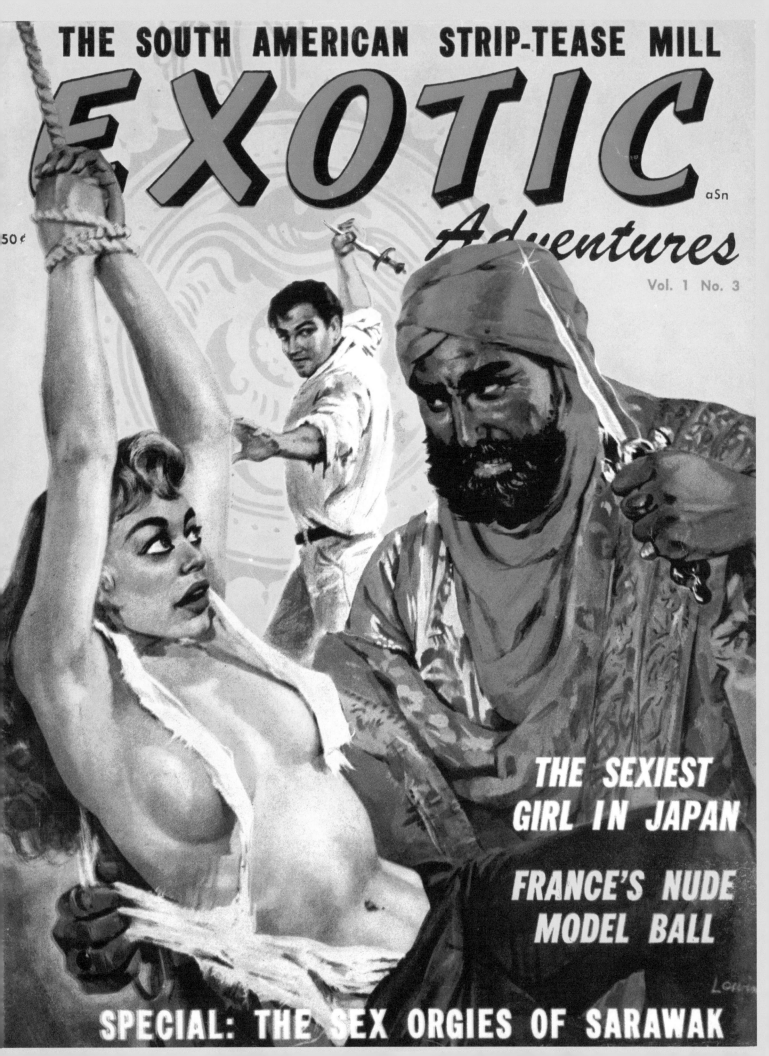

SAFARI OF DEATH

SHE WANTED HER FAT, UGLY HUSBAND OUT OF THE WAY. SHE ALSO WANTED HIS MONEY. BUT MOST OF ALL... SHE WANTED HER LOVER TO HELP HER.

by

Leon Kaiser

as told to Stan Hollis

IT WAS LIKE a scene in a dream. There was the lion, bounding out of the brush and heading straight for Barrett, who didn't see it—and, fifty feet away, Barrett's voluptuous young wife stood by, with a rifle in her hands, and watched, just watched! She wasn't making the slightest attempt to save her husband's life. In fact, I thought I heard her silvery, tinkling laughter!

We were camped near the Benoue River in the French Cameroons, just across from Rei Bouba. We were following down a report that lions had been seen in the neighborhood, and we hoped to bag a couple to put up on our walls at home. What was a safari if we didn't come home with a lion head to show for it?

(Continued on page 18)

17

And there was our lion now. But Barrett, who was fat, fifty-five, and hard of hearing, was looking off in the other direction. And Lois Barrett was quite coolly letting her husband meet tawny death!

I was a couple of hundred yards away, too far for an accurate shot. My wife Ethel was on the other side of the river, and our white hunter, Peter Laird, was even further from Barrett than I was. Only Lois Barrett had a clear shot at the charging beast—and she wasn't doing a damned thing to save him!

"Barrett!" I shouted. *"Watch out! Lion!"*

No use. He couldn't hear me. The lion was no more than twenty feet from him now. I ran furiously across the flat plain, gasping in deep breaths of the 110-degree air, yelling and hoping against hope that I would be in a position to take a shot before the lion reached Barrett.

There wasn't even time to hope. The lion caught up with the astonished Barrett, soaring in one graceful bound through the air to drag him to the ground. The lions of French Equatorial Africa are not the tame, sleepy beasts of Tanganyika or South Africa's Kruger National Park. Here, they are alarmingly ferocious beasts. I got a good view of their ferocity, too. The lion literally ripped Barrett to shreds in the few seconds of the attack. One mighty swipe of the paw disembowelled him, and his throat was severed in one growling snap.

Then—and only then—did Lois Barrett wake up. She hoisted her .375 and blazed away at the feasting lion. When I was close enough, I joined in. Within moments, Peter Laird was on the scene to finish the beast off. And then we took a look at what was left of Barrett. He lay flat, with his

intestines spilling out and his throat bitten through. Laird, whitefaced, was muttering that he couldn't understand it, that this was the first time he had ever lost a client, that this could never have happened if everyone had been alert.

I looked away from the corpse, sickened. I couldn't meet Lois Barrett's eyes, because I knew I'd see an adulterous come-hither smile in them. If it hadn't been murder, it was the closest thing to it. She had deliberately refused to shoot—when she, and she alone, could have saved her husband's life. It had been cold-blooded murder, whatever excuse she tried to give …

Our ill-fated safari had gotten under way a month earlier, in Paris. Ethel and I were there for a sort of second honeymoon—after six years of marriage, we were coming uncomfortably close to the brink of divorce, and we had decided on the European trip as a final measure that would either bring us closer together or else put finish to what hadn't been a very successful marriage.

We met the Barretts, George and Lois, one night in the Lido. They were an improbable couple. Barrett was heavy-set and balding, well into his middle fifties, with extra chins and a pot-belly. His wife Lois was about twenty-eight, a radiant long-legged blonde with big breasts and bedroom eyes. The blonde hair, I was later to discover, was natural—and the bedroom eyes weren't just a tease act.

It struck me immediately that she had married him for his money, of course. Barrett didn't look like he was in good enough physical shape to satisfy a female hellion like Lois. My guess on that score turned out to be one hundred percent accurate.

The Barretts were unhappy that night because they were due to leave in a week on a safari to French Equatorial Africa, and the couple they were supposed to go with had just backed out because of an unexpected pregnancy. Everything was all arranged, the equipment purchased and the guides

hired, but they didn't want to go alone.

"How about you two?" George Barret asked. "Think you'd care to go on a safari with us?"

I wasn't too keen on the idea—until I got a look at Lois Barrett's face. She was silently pleading with me to say yes. I frowned a moment. My relations with Ethel had been deteriorating during the past few days, and we had stopped sleeping together again. It looked pretty obvious that we were heading for a final smashup. And I interpreted the look on Lois' face to mean that she was available, if I was interested.

Well, I thought, I probably *would* be interested. We had the cash to afford a safari—I'm pretty high up on one of the television networks' list of executives—and we had the time. So off we went with George and Lois Barrett to Africa.

We started in Fort Archambault, principal town of French Equatorial Africa, where we picked up our jeeps and our white hunter. Peter Laird was not the standard glamor-boy white hunter of the movies. He was a short, wiry little man with a heavy beard, a hook nose, and one shoulder higher than the other—but he knew his job.

After a couple of days in Fort Archambault we set out on the trail, ferrying across the Salamat River and striking northeast toward Lake Iro. We had our first big hunting day at the village of Madecongo, in the Territory of Chad. We pitched our tents in a grove of sausage trees where it was 112 degrees in the shade, and brought down some waterbuck before moving on.

Forty miles to the east, in the Chad village of Kyabe, we met the Ubangi platter-lipped women. Several days later, near Makhounda, we lashed canoes together and crossed the clear, rocky Barya river. We passed through the Guidari region, ruled by a gigantic potentate named Chief Gabaroun who, we were told, had 87 wives and 132 children. Moving on, we headed for the mountains of the Cameroons, a French trusteeship adjoining Chad.

Here, in the plains country of Rei Bouba, we settled down to do our real hunting.

So much for the bare geographical details of where we went. Much more interesting is Lois Barrett's part in the safari.

Before we left Paris, Lois and I had no chance to get together. But our first night in Fort Archambault, she made up for all the lost time. We were staying in a tiny hotel, a dingy place whose woodwork crawled with repulsive insects. It was near dinner time. Ethel and I had had a quarrel that afternoon at the airport, and she had dressed for dinner and gone flouncing out of the room to leave me by myself. I was stripped to the waist and shaving when there was a knock on the door.

I opened it. Lois Barrett stood there. It was the first moment we had been alone together.

She smiled warmly as she closed the door behind her. She was wearing an informal bathrobe sort of garment, and as the door closed she let the robe slip to the floor. She was nude underneath it.

"I've waited so long for this, Leon!"

"Do you think it's safe?" I asked, eyeing the creamy loveliness of her body. Compared to her, Ethel was thin and angular. Lois' breasts were high and full, without a trace of droop. Her hips curved invitingly. "There's no way of locking the door," I said. "And suppose George or Ethel—"

"They're both downstairs having cocktails," she said. "I checked. We have half an hour, at least, before they'll miss us. Let's make the most of it."

We certainly did. She was like some fierce panther as she clung to me, her teeth nipping my shoulder. "God," she breathed. "I haven't felt this way in years. George is practically impotent. Again, darling! Again!"

We only had half an hour together that time. But under the intimate conditions of the safari, we had more and more opportunities. Once, after both my wife and her husband had dropped

off to sleep, we left our tents and made love under a bright moon. Another time, Lois was bathing in a nearby stream early one morning when I stole up behind her and embraced her nakedness.

Through all of our hundreds of miles of trek in Africa's dark heart, Lois and I found ways of getting together. Ethel did not seem to notice, or if she did she kept her opinions to herself. Naturally, Ethel and I did not have marital relations, not when I was devoting all my energies to Lois, but that was far from unusual in our marriage. As for George Barrett, he did not indicate that he knew he was being cuckolded. Maybe he didn't care. Maybe he was simply glad that someone else was relieving him of the responsibility of making love to his wife—a responsibility for which he definitely lacked the proper equipment.

I told Lois that Ethel and I would probably get a divorce as soon as we returned to America. "What about you?" I asked her. "You aren't going to stay married to George forever, are you? Wouldn't he give you a divorce if you wanted one?"

She shook her head. "He hates scandal. He would never agree to a divorce. But I'll find some way, darling. Some way to let us be together always."

At the time, I couldn't think of a better fate than to spend the rest of my life in the sack with Lois Barrett. She was everything a woman ought to be, I thought. Never before had I known a woman so passionate, so lovely— and so available. Old George Barrett couldn't live forever, I told myself. Maybe he had a bad heart, or diabetes, or something like that.

George didn't have much longer to live when I thought those thoughts. But it wasn't a heart attack that had carried him away—

LOIS AND I had made love the night before the lion hunt at the Benoue River. We had embraced each other

in a vacant tent, while the others were skinning the day's kill. But even though it was as splendid a session as any that had gone before, I felt a touch of regret as I fondled Lois' ripe breasts and smooth thighs. For Ethel was becoming more affectionate again. Whether it was jealousy at work or not, I didn't know—but she was talking about another reconciliation. Our marriage could be saved, now—if I wanted it to be. But, with a choice between Lois and Ethel, it was impossible to think of wanting to save the marriage. All I wanted was Lois—all night, every night.

And then came the day of the lion hunt. A blazing hot day, with even the native bearers wilting. A lion had been flushed; it was somewhere in the scrub, skulking around, with its mate. But Peter Laird didn't know where, and so we fanned out all over, with instructions to stay on our toes.

And then the mighty beast came loping down at George Barrett, while Lois stood by and laughed—

Of course, I thought, and I felt chilled despite the blistering heat. George had refused to give her a divorce. So she was taking this way of getting rid of him! Any desire I might have had for Lois vanished forever in that moment. She was no longer a human being to me, just a splendidly designed machine for sex, with no more emotions than a robot. I knew I could never love such a woman, no matter how tempting her breasts and body might be.

There was general hubbub after Barrett was killed. Peter Laird took charge, and the body was borne away by the natives. Lois looked dazed.

The white hunter said to her, "Mrs. Barrett, will you be coming back to camp with us now?"

"In a few minutes," she said. "Mr. Kaiser will bring me back. I—just want to be by myself a little while."

Laird shrugged and the procession trudged away, leaving Lois and I alone. Ethel had already acrossed the river, and so she knew nothing of what had happened. Her party would not be

returning for some time yet.

Lois smiled, throwing back her shoulders to make her large breasts stand out against her shirt. "At last we're free, darling! I'll inherit George's money, and you can divorce that hag Ethel, and there'll be just the two of us, always—"

I shook my head, dumbfounded. "You just stood there and let the lion kill him! You could have fired, but you didn't, Lois!"

She nodded. "Of course. What simpler way was there to get rid of him? After all, he stood in the way of our love, Leon—"

"You think I'd marry you—*now?*"

Her expression changed. "What do you mean?" she said in an edgy voice.

"You virtually murdered your husband," I said thinly. "Do you really think I'd want to marry a murderess?"

"But—we had to get rid of him, Leon—"

"You killed him!"

"All right," she said quietly. "I killed him. What of it? Divorce Ethel and we can get married. We can have each other *legally!* Every night!"

"No go, Lois. I'm going to stay married to Ethel. I certainly wouldn't leave her for an amoral slut like you."

Fury blazed in her eyes. She lifted her rifle and for one moment I thought she was going to gun me down—until I saw she was aiming the big gun past me.

I turned to see her target.

It was Ethel—my wife!

Ethel was crossing the river, coming back early. She had some sort of trophy in her boat, and she was calling out to us, unaware of the day's bloody tragedy. And Lois had her square in the sights!

"I'll save you the trouble of getting a divorce," she muttered. "And then you'll *have* to marry me!"

"Lois—*no!*"

I charged forward, deflecting the gun upward. The bullet crashed harmlessly into the air. Then, seizing the rifle from Lois' hand, I swung it round and in blind fury smashed her down with the stock!

My blow caught her along the side of the head. She fell, blood streaming down her cheek. Shaking her head dazedly, she tried to rise, but she was groggy. My sanity returned as I saw the welling blood matting her delicate blonde hair. For an instant I even forgot that she had murdered her husband and tried to kill my wife. She was hurt, and I had done it.

Then I heard a snarl—and, a moment later, a distant shriek from Ethel.

Whirling, I saw the lioness charge. She had been lurking in the brush, and now—incited, perhaps, by the scent of blood on the air—had come bounding forward. I leaped out of the way just in time. But Lois, dazed, half-unconscious on the ground, could not escape.

The slaughter was quick. The lioness' first swipe ripped open only the front of Lois' shirt, baring for the last time those round breasts I had so passionately kissed only the night before. Then the beast ripped and slashed at Lois' silken throat. Blood spouted crazily.

Reeling to minimum firing distance, I pumped bullet after bullet into the hungry lioness, and when my rifle was empty I rushed forward to crash it down again and again on the tawny beast that still crouched over Lois' half-devoured form …

THERE WAS no question of further safari after that. We returned to Fort Archambault and there George and Lois Barrett were buried. No one but Ethel and I knew the true story of how they met their deaths.

Ethel and I managed a reconciliation, and today, three years afterward, we are more happily married than ever before. My interlude of adultery with Lois Barrett is just a memory now. But it's a memory that will remain with me always—the memory of a blonde temptress with fire in her veins and steel in her heart, who met bloody death under the blazing sun of French Equatorial Africa.

The end

89-40 493

I WAS A **TANGIER'S SMUGGLER**

ANTONIO LUCETTA

by
Donald Gorman
as told to Lloyd Lawrence

THERE WAS PLENTY OF MONEY TO BE MADE BY BLACK-MARKETING CIGARETTES FROM TANGIERS TO ITALY. THERE WAS ALSO DEATH AND IMPRISONMENT FOR THOSE WHO DIDN'T MAKE IT.

OUR LITTLE MOTOR LAUNCH purred smoothly through the Mediterranean waters, heading outward from the international zone of Tangier. A gentle haze hovered over the waters—a haze that shielded us from the trigger-happy gunboats of the Spanish customs officials.

But still there was a coppery taste in my mouth from sheer tension. As of the past hour, I was a full-fledged smuggler. And if a customs gunboat decided to challenge us, we had the choice of making a run for it (and getting blown out of the water) or of letting ourselves get caught redhanded (thereby insuring ourselves of a couple of years or more in a Spanish prison.)

We were bound for Italy, a three-day journey, with a cargo consisting of a thousand cases of American cigarettes. Not very sinister, you say? Well, maybe not as gaudy as smuggling

(Continued on next page)

23

heroin, I'll admit—but just as illegal, in this part of the world.

We also had one other item of cargo on board: our employer's Moroccan mistress. She was down below, getting some rest.

As I stood alone on deck, keeping an eye peeled for the customs boys, I had to smile at the thought of being a smuggler. I had been plenty of things in the ten years since World War II had ended, but this was the shadiest.

I fought in Europe during the War, and decided to stay in England after V-E Day. I knocked around in all sorts of odd jobs, some of them on this side of the law and some of them on the other, and one day in 1954 I happened to become the owner of an ex-naval Fairmile motor launch that had been roughly converted to look like a yacht.

"Why not pick up some cash smuggling out of Tangier?" someone suggested, and I was hooked. I got together a crew of five, all of them ex-Royal Navy men who hadn't been able to make a go of it in civilian life, and off we went to the fabled city of the Casbah.

Tangier is a free port. Ships of any nation can unload any kind of cargo at all there, without paying duty or undergoing inspection. A highly organized smuggling trade operates out of Tangier, therefore—ferrying goods from the free port to the nations along the Mediterranean coast. The smuggling rings specialize in such desired items as gems, coffee, watches, drugs, currency, antibiotic drugs, and gold—as well as American cigarettes, which are heavily dutied in Europe, and which so many Europeans became addicted to, thanks to the presence of G.I.s during the '40s.

American cigarettes are imported by Tangier at $40 a case. Off the coast of France, Italy, or Spain those same cases bring $80 apiece from the black market wholesalers, who peddle their goods to small local vendors at around $160 a case. So both sets of middlemen rake off a 100% profit, and even with the double gouge the local retailers still can undersell the legally imported item, as well as the stiffly-taxed local brands.

We were one hour out of Tangier with our cargo. I had obtained the job by going to an office in the new European quarter of Tangier, the office of a sleek, suave Latin who ran a so-called "Maritime Agency."

This smooth operator introduced me to an olive-skinned Lebanese who represented the black-market organization in Italy, and we talked terms. He had a thousand cases of American cigarettes sitting on the dock in Tangier Bay—an investment of $40,000. He could double his money if he could get the cigarettes to the Italian Riviera. Did I know of any small craft that might be going that way?

I said I did. I said a small craft could be hired through me.

"At what price?" my Lebanese man wanted to know.

I puffed at my cigarette—a Chesterfield—and through a thick cloud of smoke said, "Fifteen percent of purchase price." It was the standard fee, that I had been told to ask by more experienced hands.

He scowled at me and tried to bargain in the true Levantine fashion. "$4500 is more what I had in mind—not $6000."

I knew what happened to new men who broke the rigid price barrier. Blowing smoke casually in his face, I said, "You've heard the price. Now, if you'll excuse me, I have some other people to see—"

"$5000."

I started to get up. He said hastily, "All right, then, American. You bleed me, but I'll give you what you ask. On one condition."

I frowned. "What's the condition?"

"I have a—female friend here in Morocco," he said with an oily smile. "Quite attractive. I would like you to take her to the destination as well."

"A woman on board? It's a small ship—"

"She will be no trouble. She is well behaved."

"And suppose the customs men catch us?"

His face darkened. "I have more faith in you than that, Captain Gorman. $6000 plus fuel—if you will take the girl with you."

In the end, I agreed. I didn't like the idea of having a passenger on board, but on the other hand I didn't have that much confidence in my haggling abilities. So it was all arranged. We would leave the following night, with the girl and with the cigarettes, and when we delivered the goods the Lebanese's partner would give us $6000 in cash, plus an allowance for our diesel fuel—no skimpy amount, on a round-trip journey of nearly 2000 miles. We fixed our rendezvous, agreed on signals, and made out ship's papers for Valetta, Malta. It was the standard dodge for a ship leaving Tangier—"Reporting to Malta for further instructions," was all we would tell anyone, and if we were lucky we would be believed.

The next day we loaded our yacht. None of the Moroccan officials who are stationed in Tangier seemed to care. Everything was open and above-board, since presumably we intended to pay duty on our cargo when we unloaded it in Italy.

Around twilight, our passenger showed up, in the company of Mario, the Italian pilot sent by the Lebanese to guide our craft to the rendezvous. Mario was short and squat, with heavy jowls and a drooping black mustache badly stained by nicotine. He went below almost immediately to inspect his quarters.

Meanwhile *we* inspected the girl. She was a dusky Moroccan beauty with black hair that fell in loose tresses to her shoulders. She couldn't have been more than twenty-one or twenty-two, and she couldn't speak a word of

English. I found myself envying the little Lebanese. The girl—I never found out her name—was a long-legged lovely, with skin the color of light chocolate. She wore a low-cut western-style dress that revealed the creamy upper hemispheres of her full, swelling breasts. She was a breath-taking sight. I ordered Sinkwich, our Number Two mate, to take her below to her cabin while we finished loading.

It was past sundown by the time we shoved off. I spent the first hour in a state of nerves. For the first time, I realized what risks I was running for the sake of this cargo. If we were caught, we might spend the rest of our lives rotting away behind bars. Law is notoriously vague in Mediterranean countries. We could be jailed without trial and then simply forgotten about for ten or twenty years, and there would be no way we could protest—for who would listen?

Even so, it was worth it. $6000 for a three-day trip, and 25% of the fee was mine as skipper—$1500. My five cohorts would each draw $900. Not bad for a few days' work. At that rate I could earn as much in a month as I did in a whole year in England, and none of it would be taxed.

I spent the first hour alone on the deck as we passed through the Straits of Gibraltar. The Spanish customs men at that time came from two directions—south from Algeciras and north from Ceuta—and some-times they preferred machine-gunning to asking questions. The harbor in Tangier Bay is lined with derelict hulls rotting away—"Death Row," that district is called. The ships belonged to smugglers who didn't quite make it through the Straits.

But luck was with us. No customs boats appeared. An hour and a half after leaving, Sinkwich came up from below, and tapped me on the shoulder.

"Our passenger wants to see you, Skipper." He was leering gaily. "Have fun, old man!"

I nodded. "Keep an eye peeled for the customs boats. I'll be back up here as soon as I can."

"Take your time!" he called after me.

I WENT belowdecks and made my way through the narrow companionway to the cabin where we had put the Lebanese's mistress. I knocked.

"*Chi va la'?*" she asked in Italian, repeating it in French: "Who's there?"

My French vocabulary is bigger than my Italian one, but my pronuncia-tion is lousy in French. I said in Italian, "*Il capitano.*"

She opened the door. She was wearing a filmy nightgown and a big smile. A moment later, she swept her arms upward briskly and she was wearing just the smile.

Her body was flawless: high, proud, red-tipped breasts, a softly rounded belly, gently curving hips. Her skin was delicately pale—the finest sort an Arab woman can have. She looked like a magnificent animal.

"I was lonely," she said, locking the cabin door behind me.

For an uneasy moment I wondered whether there was some trick involved in all this. But I didn't stop to argue. She pirouetted into my arms, pressing her breasts up against me as I fondled the firm roundnesses of her buttocks.

"Their hotel is all the way across town."

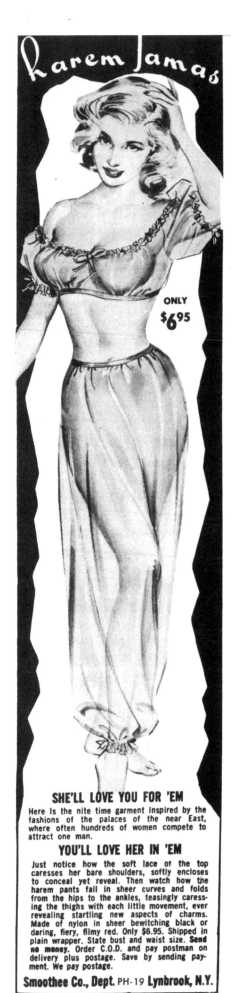
Then she drew me down to the bed, giggling in anticipation of pleasure, glueing her mouth to mine, taking my hands and making them move over every part of her body until she virtually quivered with frenzy.

She was an expert in lovemaking: I've never had it better, either before or since. I think she was one of those girls who is spotted at an early age, say twelve or thirteen, and taken to the Tangier Casbah to be instructed in the arts of love—and then, at eighteen, after an intensive five-year course, is sold to some well-heeled Lothario for his private use. This girl had obviously had the postgraduate course too. She could do everything in the books, and a couple of Arab specialties I had never even thought of.

The next three hours were just one long happy tumult of heaving breasts and writhing pelvises, of un-dulating hips and bouncing buttocks. We didn't do any talking in Italian or French or any other language except the language of our bodies, but that conversation was a doozie.

And then, finally, I remembered I was skipper of a smuggling launch. I detached myself from her ardent grasp, got back into my clothes, and mumbled clumsy Italian apologies as I backed out of the cabin.

Sinkwich was still on deck. "No sign of trouble?" I asked him.

"All's well, skipper. How was it belowdecks?"

"All was well down there," I said, tightening my belt a little.

THE NEXT two days passed quickly—too quickly, from one point of view, and not quickly enough, for another. I would have loved to spend months at sea with the Lebanese's Moroccan belle—but, contrariwise, I was anxious to reach our rendezvous and get rid of our cargo.

We dodged some bad weather round the Gulf of Lyons by skirting east of the Balearics, and that put us a little bit ahead of schedule. I managed to fit two more sessions with the Moroccan into my personal schedule. She was distributing her favors impar-tially among everybody on board. My crew, being Englishmen, did not boast about their "conquest," but I could tell from the smug expressions on their faces that it wasn't only the Skipper who was rolling in the hay below-decks. Apparently the Lebanese's little girl was a very hot cookie who needed constant satisfaction to keep herself happy—and with a boatload of willing men, she must have been extremely happy indeed.

On the third day, we were getting pretty close to shore and to our rendez-vous, four miles south of Portofino on the Riviera. The ship was blacked out, and I had forbidden smoking on deck. I scanned the horizon tensely, looking for sign of a customs boat from Genoa. If anything, the Italian customs men have become stricter than the Spanish boys, and the sentences are stiff: it's an automatic seven-day jail term for being caught buying or selling even a single pack of bootleg American butts, and getting nabbed with a thousand cases would be very very bad—a lo-o-o-ng jail term with no hope of help from the local American consul, who isn't going to break his back to bail out a smuggler.

Mario, our pilot, came on deck with a cigarette dangling lighthteart-edly from his lips.

"I thought I told everybody there was to be no smoking on deck this close to shore!" I snapped.

Mario grinned and punched my shoulder cheerfully. "Donta you worry, Skipper. My boss, he gotta deal with the custom polizia. They look the other way and my boss put a couple kilos oil in da custom launch diesel fuel when he expects da cargo."

"I'm still not taking any chances," I said. "Douse the cigarette."

He grumbled a bit, but finally tossed it over the rail. Neither my pre-cautions nor shoreside sabotage helped us, though. Maybe Mario's boss forgot to dump sugar into the fuel this time. Anyway, around 2 AM we heard the sound of a launch coming toward us. The thick coastal haze made it almost impossible for us to see them—but they could see us, it seemed.

A Genoese customs launch—coming right at us—and we had a thousand cases of undeclared cigarettes belowdecks!

Suddenly all hands were on deck. Mario couldn't understand it.

"What should we do, Skipper?" I was asked. "Make a break for it?"

I shook my head. "That would be sheer suicide. Let's try to bluff them out."

A few moments later the launch pulled up alongside us. An Italian customs officer signalled that he was coming aboard. He was short and stocky, with a grim, efficient look about him.

He wanted to see our papers. I produced them. The papers said we were en route to Malta from Tangier, but we were hundreds of miles north of our alleged destination. How come, he asked? What was our cargo? What were we trying to pull, anyway. Maybe we'd all better come ashore and have a talk with the *polizia*.

I cursed the day I had ever gone into the smuggling game. I vowed that if I ever got out of jail in Genoa, I'd spend the rest of my life in virtuous pursuits. I had dismal visions of myself sojourning in Marassi Prison till some time in 1980.

Suddenly Mario interposed himself between the customs inspector and myself, and began to talk in a stream of Italian so rapid I could hardly follow more than every tenth word. I heard him repeat the name of our Lebanese employer several times—and he made a couple of obscene gestures, too. The customs man merely frowned.

"*Un momento!*" Mario cried. "Wait a second!" He dashed down belowdecks.

He returned a moment later with our passenger. The girl wore only a filmy negligee through which her high, pointed breasts were plainly visible, and she was giving the customs man the eye. He lost his frown

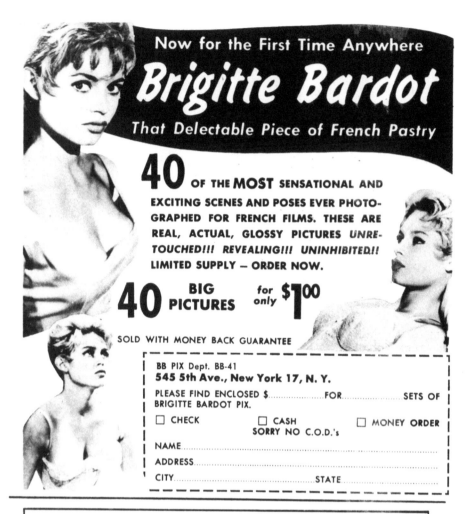

in half a second. She opened a top button, jutting the rounded swells of her breasts forward. She was square in the spotlight field of the customs boat, and she was a lovely sight.

The customs man nodded thoughtfully, stepped forward, spun her around to examine her hips and buttocks as if buying a prize horse. Then he went belowdecks with her.

Mario grinned. "We were almost in very serious trouble, but now we will be all right," he announced.

The customs man was belowdecks more than an hour, while we sat around on deck, locking our hands nervously. Finally he came up, alone. He was smiling.

"Quest' e' un miracolo," he exclaimed. "That woman is a miracle!"

He climbed over the rail and into his boat. "I did not see you, *signori. Buona sera.*"

And the customs launch vanished into the haze.

We let out our breaths in one enormous collective sigh of relief. Mario merely snickered. "Some-a da customs men, they pretty corrupt," he exclaimed. "We were lucky tonight."

WE HUNG offshore at the rendezvous for another hour, and then we heard the sound of oars. A fishing boat was approaching through the mist. When it pulled up, two Italians in city clothes jumped aboard, nodded to Mario, and congratulated me on our narrow escape.

"How did you do it?" they asked.

I shrugged. The last thing I wanted to do was to tell them the truth, for fear the Lebanese might find out and be jealous. "I argued with him and he lost," I said simply.

At their instructions, we brought the yacht closer to shore, until we were no more than half a mile from the beach, and we could see the people in the windows of the passing coast train from Genoa. Then we began to unload into the fishing boats. The job took four hours, and everyone smoked and chattered as the cases came up through the hatches and were passed over the side. I was handed a fat envelope full of hundred-dollar bills. I counted through it: we had all our money, to the penny.

It was eight in the morning by the time the job was done. We were in broad daylight by now. The girl was long since gone, leaving unforgettable memories behind. Our ship unloaded, our fee paid, we turned about and laid a course back to Tangier.

I had lost eight pounds on the trip, and picked up a few new gray hairs. But I was $1500 richer—not to mention the memories I now had, priceless ones, of that hot-blooded Moroccan lass.

Despite all my vows of quitting while I was ahead, I contracted for a new smuggling trip as soon as we returned to Tangier. We completed it without incident, and as a matter of fact at no time in my eighteen-month smuggling career did I again have a serious brush with customs officials. On the other hand, never again did we have so lovely—and so willing—a passenger on board. When I sold the yacht and retired from the Tangier trade, late in 1955, I had a nest egg of better than $30,000. I'm investing it in smart stocks now—and some day, when I'm rich enough, I'm going to go back to Tangier and buy me a lovely Moroccan lassie all my own.

The end

"No really, we all think it's kinda cute the way your checks bounce!"

ATTACKED BY MONSTER CRABS

CAN YOU THINK OF A MORE HORRIBLE WAY TO DIE, THAN TO BE TORN TO SHREDS BY A HORDE OF MONSTER CRABS? I CAN'T! BECAUSE IT ALMOST HAPPENED TO ME...

by

Dave Callahan

"THIS IS THE PLACE," Pamela said. "We'll be all alone here. Nobody ever comes here but me."

We climbed out of our outboard motorboat and up onto the sandy shore. We had come ashore on a tiny mangrove-dotted inlet along the coast of British Honduras, a little ways north of Belize, the capital. The place was idyllic. And we had the whole beach to ourselves, Pamela and I. I was looking forward to a long afternoon of love with this busty daughter of a British diplomat. I wasn't prepared for the nightmare events that would take place that afternoon.

"Do you come here very often?" I asked as we beached the boat.

She grinned enigmatically. "Whenever I feel the need to get away from the town."

(Continued on page 32)

"You come alone?"

"Sometimes," she said. "Unless I have company. *Interesting company*, like you, David."

Hand in hand, we climbed up the beach bank. It was a warm, muggy day; Pamela was wearing a man's white shirt whose buttons barely managed to hold back the magnificent thrust of her bosom, and a pair of khaki trousers that clung tightly to her hips and thighs. Overhead, the hot sun was burning its way through the thick clouds. I spread a blanket for the two of us. There were two bottles of local rum in the boat, for refreshments, and we had forgotten them.

"I'll go back to the boat and get them," I said. When I reached the boat, I scooped up the bottles and looked up-beach. Pamela was peeling off her blouse. She had nothing on underneath. I ogled her gently swaying breasts appreciatively as I approached. She unbuttoned the trousers, kicked them off, and stood lovely and nude before me.

Her body was evenly tanned—she had no telltale strips of white across her middle. From her throat down past her full, round breasts to her beautifully-sculpted legs, she was a splendid golden-brown. She shook her red hair out in the air.

"Come—get undressed and let's have a swim first," she said in those crisp British accents that sounded so out of place in this primitive Central American country. "After we've bathed, we can enjoy ourselves on the blanket."

Smiling, I said, "You go ahead and get your feet wet while I'm opening the bottle. I want a nip of rum before I get into the water."

She nodded and went skipping down to the edge of the beach, where the Caribbean waters lapped against the sand. As she ran I watched the smooth play of muscles in her back and buttocks. If ever a girl had been made for love, I thought, Pamela had.

She waded out into the shallow water while I busied myself with the corkscrew-attachment of my knife. Finally I got the bottle open and took a deep, tingling pull of the flavorsome British Honduras-style rum. Glancing downbeach, I saw Pamela gleefully splashing around. She was swimming alongshore toward a projecting cove over to the east.

I unbuckled my belt and started to slip out of my trousers. Suddenly I heard screams.

"David! David! Help—*the crabs—the crabs—*"

I shaded my eyes and looked downbeach for her. She was almost completely hidden around the cove; all I could see of her was her body from the breasts upward. She was leaping around wildly in the shallow water some thirty feet offshore.

Grabbing up the unopened bottle of rum to use as a weapon, I sprinted toward the water. "What's happening?" I yelled. "What's the trouble?"

"The crabs!" she shrieked. *"The monster crabs!"*

Half stumbling over myself in my hurry, I reached the edge of the shore. There was Pamela, off shore in water no higher than her lovely knees—and monster crabs a foot across were leaping up out of the water, gnashing their ugly pincers at her nude form! The water seemed to boil with their hideous forms. There must have been hundreds of the crabs, swarming up from their slumbers in the mud.

She was screaming in utter mindless panic. I could see a bloody gash along one arm, another just beneath one jouncing breast. She was doing a wild dance, a death-dance, and the water around her was stained with red.

And I heard the sound the crabs made: the dull, ominous *clack-clack* sound of heavy pincers cracking together.

Pamela was trying to beat the monsters off with her hands, but they were slashing her mercilessly on hip and thigh and arm and belly and buttock and every other part of her body they could reach.

Raising my bottle high as a club, I waded out into the water, conscious that my unprotected nakedness was terribly vulnerable to the attack of the crabs. I didn't care. I had to save Pamela…

THE PICNIC that turned into bloody nightmare took place only one day after I had first met Pamela Hunt. I was in the sleepy capital of British Honduras on legal business. It seems that in 1940 a well-to-do family had fled from Belgium before Hitler's legions, and had taken refuge in Belize, British Honduras. After the end of the war, one branch of the family emigrated to New York, the rest staying behind in Central America. Now, a wealthy member of the New York branch had died, and I had been sent down here to seek out the beneficiaries of his will.

I hadn't been in Belize more than an hour when I met Pamela Hunt. Having checked in at my hotel, I stepped out into the quiet street for a look round town. Turning a corner, I bumped into a tall and well-built white woman about twenty-five years old.

"Sorry," I said automatically. I had almost knocked her down.

"You mustn't turn corners like that," she said with an impish grin. "Down here nobody's ever in a hurry, you see. Life moves slowly."

My eyes went up and down her lush body. "I'll be more careful next time—but it certainly was a pleasure to bump into you, Miss—Miss—"

"Hunt. Pamela Hunt. My father's a member of the local diplomatic corps. I've been living here eight years, and it's wonderful to see a strange face. A strange *male* face."

That was the beginning. Pamela volunteered to show me around town—there wasn't much to see—and then we stopped in for a drink at a native rum-shop. She was terribly bored she told me, but her mother was dead and her father needed her to serve as hostess in diplomatic functions and the like. I was sympathetic. Sympathetic enough to find myself seated next to her in a trim little Jaguar, heading out of the heart of town and out to a handsome colonial mansion some five miles away. It formed a sharp contrast with the shoddy little native hovels. This, Pamela said, was her home.

"Daddy" wasn't home, it seemed. We went inside, were served cocktails by one of Daddy's servants, and then went upstairs to Pamela's room. She closed the door and was out of her clothes an instant later. I hadn't expected things to happen quite this way.

She was no virgin, but it had been a

long time since she had made love, and I got the benefit of all the stored-up passion inside her. Her body was fantastic, and she used it well. Maybe she hadn't had much experience, but she was a natural bed-partner all the same.

Later, as we lay utterly spent in each other's arms, she asked me how long I was going to be here

"A week or two," I told her. "As soon as I've settled the business of the will, I'll have to fly back to New York."

"Only a week or two?" she pouted. "We must make the most of it, then! What are you doing tomorrow?"

"In the morning I'm seeing the Schultz nephews," I said. "I'm free all afternoon, though."

"Splendid! There's a wonderful little inlet up the coast from Belize. You need a motorboat to get to it, and hardly anyone around here has a motorboat. We do, though. I'll ask Daddy to let me have the boat tomorrow, and we'll have a little outing, shall we?"

She insisted that I stay for dinner and meet Daddy—he was a stuffed shirt who didn't say three words to me beyond the formalities—and later that evening she drove me back to the hotel in town, agreeing to pick me up at noon the next day.

I couldn't wait. I dreamed of her that night—of this ravishing girl stuck away in a dreary Central American colony that was half jungle and half swamp, waiting for lovers to come. I even developed some fantasies of marrying her and taking her back to civilization with me. The more I thought about that, the more I liked the idea. I had survived for thirty-two years without getting hooked into matrimony, but this girl had everything: beauty, brains, culture, and just the right touch of exoticism to make her something worth showing off in New York.

The next morning I held my first conference with the Schultz heirs, but my mind wasn't really on what I was doing, and the meeting was inconclusive. At noon, the little red Jaguar was waiting outside the hotel for me.

I kissed her hello as if I'd known her for years and not just for a single day, and we drove down to the harbor, where she turned the Jag over to a native servant and boarded the motorboat that took us to her secret inlet.

I've already told the next part—of how we beached the boat, how Pamela stripped to the buff and went down to the shore to wade. It was then that the hellish nightmare began, the nightmare that has haunted me every night in the three years since that day…the nightmare of attacking crabs…

PAMELA'S beautiful face was a hideous mask of sheer terror and pain as I waded toward her, slipping and sliding on the slimy mud. Evil claws flicked up from the water around her, drawing blood at every touch, and she was cut off from the shore by a solid mass of the crabs. The drifting tides had sent slicks of blood up and down the shore, and more crabs were on their way to join the attack.

I was thirty feet away from her… twenty…fifteen. My breath was coming in ragged bursts as I tried to run through the shallow water. I slipped and fell headlong; the rum-bottle dropped, and because it was the closest thing to a weapon I had, I knelt and groped in the choppy surf until I found it again.

"I'm coming, Pam!" I yelled.

"Hurry! Kill them! They're tearing me apart!"

Hot fire lanced through my left thigh and I knew I had reached the breeding ground of the crabs. I

slammed down with the bottle, hard, and something loathsome crunched. The dead crab still clung to my flesh. I brushed it away.

Pamela was surrounded by crabs now. They had almost bitten completely to the bone of her left arm; blood spurted in terrible gouts from the wound. There were deep slashes along the ripe curves of her buttocks. She was picking up the crabs and hurling them further out to sea, trying to make her way through the boiling mass of them and back to shore.

I tried to help her, smashing my bottle against them to stun them, and tossing them as far as I could. But it

"Oh, we don't have dues; thanks to the fantastic sale of picture post-cards!"

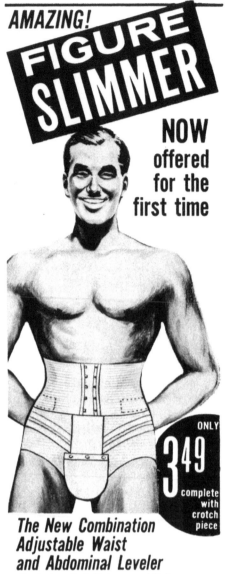
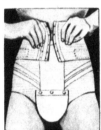
was hopeless. A naked man and a naked woman, armed only with a glass bottle between them, could not defend themselves against a seething ocean of monster crabs. I felt them nipping at my calves, my thighs, my loins…

A crab was crawling up Pamela's body. She screamed as its pincers bit into the soft flesh of her breast. I beat my way to her and wrenched the hideous creature from her body. Blood poured from the wound. I had suffered a dozen bites by now myself, and the saltwater of the Caribbean turned them into a dozen pinpoints of blazing agony.

I got my arm around Pamela's shoulders. She was sobbing hysterically, sliding and losing her footing, and she hardly knew which way to turn. I guided her, dragged her actually, while desperately trying to clear a path through the thick mass of crabs with the bottle. I might have succeeded—we were only a dozen feet off shore—but suddenly Pamela, her bare body slippery from blood and saltwater, eluded my grasp and slid beneath the surface of the water!

Instantly a swarm of black shells made for her. I groped blindly, trying to draw her up—and as I reached for her, fierce pincers seized my wrist. The sharp grip tightened…tightened… I stared at my hand as though it were a stranger's, and knew oddly that I was going to lose it. But, through a miracle, I managed to pry the crab loose. My wrist was slashed to the bone, but I had kept my hand.

Pamela, I thought. *Where is Pamela?*

Her wild thrashings had carried her five feet further out to sea. I could make out arms and legs thrusting above the water, and hundreds of blue-black giant crabs swarming round her.

I waded toward her—caught her by one arm and one leg—dragged her bodily from the water.

Crabs followed us as we made for shore. But only a few actually crawled out onto the sand. I got a good look at one, a repellent beast with busy little legs and two beady eyes flickering at me, and then I pounded the life out of it with my bottle of rum.

I fought back the temptation to collapse on the warm sand. I was completely exhausted, bleeding from twenty deep gashes. But I had to look after Pamela. Pamela who was

half drowned, Pamela whose body was mutilated by a hundred horrible slashes—

I knelt over her. She was a ghastly sight, lying facedown on the sand, with great gaping rents in her golden-brown flesh. The muscles of her back, whose play I had admired only minutes before, now stood terribly exposed to my sight where the skin had been ripped away.

I rolled her over. One full breast had been sliced practically in half by a pincer. Her belly and thighs were dreadfully ripped apart. Blood seeped from her wounds into the sand, and I knew there would be no help for her. I put my ear to her breast. There was no sound of a heartbeat. Whether she had drowned or died of loss of blood, I had no way of knowing.

Numb and shocked myself, I lifted her mutilated body and carried it back to the blanket. There, I wrapped her in it. Then I dressed, though it was hell for me. I had four serious cuts and a host of minor ones. Somehow I got Pamela's body down to the motorboat, and found my way back to Belize. There, I staggered up onto the dock and called out for help, and toppled face-forward, too weak to stay conscious any longer.

THE NEXT few days are blurred in my memory. I was taken to the local hospital, and there my wounds were bound. I spent a few days in bed with a high fever. Pamela's father came to pay me a visit, and I told him the story as it had truthfully happened: Pamela had invited me to the inlet for the day, she had gone wading and somehow blundered into a nesting-ground of giant Caribbean crabs, and they had attacked her and cut her to pieces before I could save her. He seemed to be willing to believe that. He hardly appeared to care about his daughter's bloody fate.

When I recovered from my experience, I finished up my business in Belize and flew back to the States. That was three years ago. I haven't been able to go near saltwater since. And I lay awake at night thinking of the long-limbed redhead with the calendar-girl body, who gave herself to me one night in British Honduras and who met a death of unimaginable grisliness the next day.

The end

TAHITI: LUSTY ISLAND OF UNTAMED WOMEN

EXOTIC
Adventures

aSn

Vol. 1, No. 4

50¢

A SPECIAL
SERIES OF
EXOTIC PHOTOS!

THE
CHINESE
MATA HARI

Torture in
Darkest Africa:
TRAPPED BY MAU
MAU TERROR!

NUDIST PARADISE
ON THE RIVIERA

Without warning the black-skinned killers of the jungle were upon them. There was only one way out... a fight to the death!

by
Norman Reynolds

Everyone in the British colony of Kenya knew that trouble was coming, because the Mau Mau were on the warpath and an epidemic of killings had broken out. Hardly a night went by without one of the white settlers meeting a bloody death at the hands of the enraged Kikuyu tribe, which had risen under the Mau Mau name to throw off the yoke of European domination.

My family has had land in Kenya for generations, but I had been living in America and England for most of my life. I had returned to Kenya in 1952, just after my thirtieth birthday, at the request of my uncle. He wanted me to manage a middle-sized farm near Nairobi. Having put in a spell in Korea,

(Continued on next page)

TRAPPED BY MAU MAU TERROR

They almost paid for their illicit love with their

lives the night her husband stayed away and the

dreaded Mau Mau decided to attack.

I was looking for some peace and quiet. What nobody told me was that Kenya was on the verge of a blood-bath that, for a while, threatened to make the Korean War look like a game of tiddly-winks between Oxford and Cambridge.

The night that the incident I am about to recount took place, I couldn't have been in a more vulnerable position. I was the only white man on the farm that night. My teenage cousin, who lived there with me, was out on a Mau Mau posse. We had drawn lots, and it had fallen to me to stay behind and guard the homestead. My only company that bloody night, aside from my two massive Great Danes, were three loyal natives, the cook, the house-boy, and a porter.

It had been a bad week. Just the other day, on Lower Kabete Road on the far side of Nairobi, a white man and his wife had been hacked to death. A couple of crusty old bachelor farmers had had their heads chopped of at dinner-time by their own house-boy. Chief Waruhiu, the loyal native leader known as "The African Winston Churchill," had been shot to death in his car by terrorists. A Kikuyu city councillor had been murdered. Over in Thomson's Falls, Commander Jock Mikkelson had been shredded by Mau Mau blades, and his wife horribly mutilated but not killed. And at Nanyuki an entire family, mother, father, seven-year-old daughter, six-year-old son, had been cut down. Only the girl survived, but her legs had been severed and she had been raped a dozen times. Not a pretty thing, this Mau Mau business. And if I told you of the oaths the Mau Mau took in the forest, while devouring entrails and eyeballs and genitals plucked from live goats, it would turn your stomach. Let's just say it was sheer deadly savagery, all the terror of Africa's black barbarism rolled into one.

And there I was, that night. Already more than a dozen white settlers had been murdered, and I don't know how many hundreds of loyal natives. Kenya was full of British soldiers, the jails were full of natives, settler posses roamed around in big bands looking for troublemakers, and still the killing went on. On Christmas Day a note was found pinned to the skin of a dead African, declaring perpetual war on the white man and his black supporters, and announcing that the Mau Mau would claim twelve heads before New Year's Day.

They went one over their quota. After each killing they left behind souvenirs, Mau Mau symbols—disembowled chickens, strangled cats, cows whose udders had been hacked off, sheep whose eyes had been plucked out and impaled on thorns. They weren't content to murder settlers, they wiped out farm animals as well. It was a messy business. We figured that some 90% of the million and a quarter adult Kikuyus had gone Mau Mau. They came down from the mountains, killed and looted and burned, and ran back to their hiding places.

This night that I was alone, I had an inkling that there was going to be trouble. Our farm was pretty well isolated from the rest. Just down the road a couple of miles was the Brewster farm, but they were our only neighbors. There were two of them, Mike and Sally Brewster, who had come out to Kenya from England some time in the late '40s. Mike was a red-faced, beer-swilling English type, not very long on the brains department but extremely good-natured. So good-natured, in fact, that his wife Sally had cuckolded him a few dozen times, never with me unfortunately, and if he knew about it he didn't seem to mind. She was a girl of twenty-eight or so, with flaming red hair and enormous breasts and mocking come-hither eyes.

I had settled down for the evening. The wireless was bringing in the BBC, the fire was blazing—there wasn't any electricity or central heating inside the house—and on the porch a lantern was glowing, by command of the Kenya Police Reserve. The idea was that if the lantern went out, it would be a signal that something was wrong and the inhabitants of the farm needed help.

I had mixed up a pitcher-full of Martinis, a habit I developed in America, and I had a good book open. Just a comfortable evening at home, you might say. Except that I didn't ever know when a horde of black-skinned devils would come rushing in and hack me to pieces. I had a .45 strapped to my hip and there was a hunting rifle propped up, fully loaded, at every window. Just a quiet evening at home, you see.

My cousin Hal, out riding with the posse, was due to return home at midnight. I had to hold the fort until then. Everything was quiet until along about half past nine, when Sophocles, the bigger of my two Great Danes, suddenly fetched up from his place in front of the fire and started to prick up his ears and growl.

I was alert instantly, knowing the range of his hearing. My three supposedly loyal servants were in their quarters. But you never knew when a man loyal for twenty years would suddenly turn killer.

Going to the window, I peered out into the lantern-lit darkness. I was surprised to see a jeep pulling up in front. A woman got out, looked around carefully in all directions, and sprinted toward my porch. As she passed the lantern, I could see her plainly. It was Sally Brewster. Her heavy breasts bobbed wildly as she ran.

I threw open the door, admitted her, and slammed it shut.

"Sally! What are you doing here? Has there been trouble up your way?"

"Not yet," she said, panting to get her breath. "But there's noise in the hills, as if they're going to come down to make a raid. And I was all alone—"

"Alone?" I repeated, astonished.

She nodded. "Mike's in Nairobi with some friends. He was supposed to be back at sundown. He might be dead, or"— her face hardened scornfully—"he might be lying drunk somewhere. Either way, I was alone except for our native boys, and I didn't like it. So I tacked up a note for him and came over here. Do you mind?"

"Don't be silly. I'm all alone too— I'm grateful for your company. Care for a drink?"

"Yes, please. Thanks ever so much."

I poured her a Martini and she sat down opposite me in the big chair. I had to admit she was a remarkably attractive woman. She wore jodhpurs that clung tightly to her hips and buttocks, and her breasts jutted forward from her white open-collar blouse. The red glory of her hair tumbled about her shoulders.

We had a couple of drinks, and she moved over next to me on the sofa, and I realized she was in an amourous mood. It was a devil of a situation. She kept getting closer and closer, and finally she took my hand and slipped it into the front of her blouse. She had no brassiere on, and I found myself holding one of her big breasts. The nipple, stiff and hard, pressed into my hand. She was beginning to pant. "It makes me feel relaxed when a man holds me there," she said. "With this Mau Mau thing I need to be relaxed."

Well, I didn't mind relaxing her, and I knew what would inevitably follow. But I didn't want to share the fate of that couple up near Limuru. They had been spending the evening together under similar circumstances, and there they were, naked as jaybirds, having each other on the floor, when the Wogs burst in. One of the Mau Mau boys pinned the couple together with his sword, driving the *simi* through the man, through the woman beneath him, and into the floor. That was the way they were found, dead, when the woman's husband and some friends of his came in. Man and woman were still locked together in the act of love, as well as by the sword. I didn't want to have that happen to me.

But it might have, if the attack had come twenty minutes later. As it was, I was sitting there palming those

heavy breasts, and Sally was getting hotter and hotter, when suddenly the front door was smashed open and an immense native carrying a *simi* in one hand and a club in the other came crashing in, with a short, stocky one right behind him.

Never in my life did I disentangle myself from a wench so fast. The big bruiser came straight at me, with his knife out in front of him. The other took out toward Sally. The dogs came bounding up off the hearth and got into the general confusion.

My gun was in my hand and I put a bullet into the big fellow's chest at a range of about eight feet. A .45 packs quite a wallop at that distance, and the impact knocked him back against the door. A third native, coming in, tripped over his fallen comrade, and I shot the newcomer in the middle of his face.

Meanwhile Sally had gotten up out of her seat and was struggling with the short, stocky one. He was holding her tight with one hand and had the other in the air, about to slash her with the *simi*, when Euripides, the younger of the two Great Danes, went into action. He bounded across the room, a gray-violet blur, and took off like a gazelle, soaring through the air and opening his jaws wide. He got a grip on the native's sword arm just above the wrist, and I heard a horrible

crunching sound. The sword went clattering to the floor.

For an instant I couldn't do anything, because the dog was hanging to the native's arm and I didn't want to

shoot Euripides by mistake. But then the Mau Mau swung around, lifting the great beast completely off the floor but in the process presenting his back to me. I put a shot just above his shoulders and nearly severed his head with it.

Then a fourth one came in. He saw that we had the situation pretty well in hand, and he turned, trying to get out. Sally had her gun out by this time and she winged him in the shoulder as he turned. He went toppling forward, staggered for a second on the porch. Her second shot blasted him back of the ear and he fell forward into the rose garden.

For the first time since the attack began, we had a breather of perhaps thirty seconds. I heard the sound of scuffling behind the door to the left, and I knew there were more Mau Mau around somewhere, giving trouble to the houseboy and the cook and the porter.

At least that was what I thought. But I got out into the passageway just in time to see Kungo, our cook, pick up his meat-cleaver and bury it in the

skull of Wapaga, the houseboy. Brains went spurting. So Kungo had gone Mau Mau too! He was wrestling with the cleaver, trying to get it out of Wapaga's head, fixing to cut me in half next. I started to go for him with my gun, but just then old Sophocles came bounding out, saw what was going on, and leaped for Kungo's throat. The cleaver came around and ripped into the dog's neck. Furious, I pumped two shots into Kungo, and he lay dead over the corpse of my faithful dog.

I heard a shot from the other end of the house and hurried there. Sally had nipped someone skulking in the back yard. Euripides rushed out and got his fangs into a throat out there. We heard horrid gurgling sounds, the sounds of a man's throat being ripped out.

Everything was very quiet, suddenly. Sally stood in the middle of the living-room, her breasts heaving, the smoking gun at her side. Neither of us had been touched. There were Mau Mau bodies everywhere.

"Is that the last of them?" I asked.

She shook her head. "There's one more. I wounded him but he ran into the pantry and locked himself in."

"Come on," I said.

We went into the kitchen. The pantry door was bolted from within. I had installed the inner bolt myself, to make the little closet a good hiding place in case of attack. But I hadn't intended it to be used by our attackers.

"Give me your gun," I said.

I took Sally's weapon, since mine was all but empty and she had reloaded. Standing back, I fired a shot through the oak planking. There was a groan within. A trickle of blood appeared below the door.

"That'll take care of him," I said. "We'll give him a night to bleed to death. Then I guess we'll have to take the door off its hinges to get him out."

"Suppose he comes out by himself?"

I shrugged and fired again, aiming low. There was a second groan from within, and the sound of a body falling. "He won't come out," I said.

We walked back into the living-room. The place was a bloody mess, corpses everywhere. Nahanga, our porter, the sole survivor of the three native servants, came out. His black skin was a fine shade of green.

"All over, *bwana?*" he quivered.

"All over," I said. "Where were you?"

"In the W.C., *bwana.* Fighting frights me."

I made a mental note to get rid of him next chance I had. Cowards were no use around here. "Help me clean this carrion up," I ordered him.

We got together all the Mau Mau corpses, and piled them in the front yard. The police would be along in the morning to pick the bodies up and identify them. We took the dead houseboy around back, along with the dead dog. They were on our side, and we would bury them.

It was close to eleven by the time the job of piling up the dead and mopping up the blood was finished. I sent the cowardly Nahanga to his quarters. Then I turned to face Sally. Her blouse and face were smeared with Mau Mau blood. I remembered that we had been on the verge of making love, so long ago—was it really only an hour?—before the attack. But it seemed inappropriate, I thought, to try to take up where we had left off when interrupted.

But Sally had different ideas. Her eyes were glowing and by the dim light of our fire I saw the lust smoking in them.

"You were wonderful," she breathed. "You and that wonderful dog saved my life. And if I'd stayed at my farm they would have killed me."

"I'll drive back with you now," I said. "Perhaps your husband is home, and—"

"There's no rush." Her fingers went to the collar of her blouse. The bloodstained blouse came off in a moment, and before I could speak she had unzipped her jodhpurs and had stepped out of those. She was naked.

Her body, stained with blood and beaded with sweat, was magnificent, a thing of sheer animal beauty. Her large round breasts rose and fell with the agitation of her desire. She rubbed her palms sensuously against her firm hips.

A thousand protests rose to my mind. The Mau Mau might return, her husband might come here to fetch her, my cousin Hal could come back, the police might arrive. But the glory of her body wiped out any thought of objecting. She pulled me to her and ripped the clothes from my body like an avenging fury. And there, on the floor, lying in a puddle of Mau Mau blood, we made love.

When it was over, we dressed silently. It had been a strange evening, an evening of killing and loving. I got into my jeep and drove alongside hers all the way back to her farm, and then returned to my own. I learned later that her husband *had* been drunk in Nairobi that night, and did not return until morning.

Two months later there was another Mau Mau raid on our area, and Sally Brewster was killed. She died a horrible death—the attackers slit her belly open and dragged out her bowels while she still lived, and then they cut off those splendid breasts I had fondled that evening. Some time later, her husband confessed to me that she had been in the first months of pregnancy. I often wonder if it were my child she was bearing, conceived on that night of blood and lust. I shall never know, of course. But in the two years that followed no one was more dedicated to the ultimately successful task of wiping out Mau Mau than I, and I like to think that perhaps some of the natives I helped to kill were those who had so cruelly slain Sally. Certainly she was heroic that night the Mau Mau attacked, and certainly she was splendid in her lovemaking afterward. Nowadays, with Kenya as safe as it had been in the days before the Mau Mau terror, I think longingly of her, and wonder what might have happened between us if she had lived.

The end

We stared in horror and disbelief as the High Priest of the lost tribe started to carve up the girl strapped to the statue of the Jaguar God.

by Malcolm Hunt

The native girl was not only pretty she was also greedy for the American dollar. That's when the roof fell in and she found herself the . . .

BRIDE OF THE JAGUAR GOD

THE GIRL came to us while we were excavating the La Venta site in the swampy rain forest of Southern Mexico. At La Venta, you know, worship of the Jaguar God was carried on by the long-vanished Olmecs, fifteen hundred years ago. American archeologists have dug up stupendous relics of the Jaguar God's cult, most of them at La Venta, a little island east of the Tonala River in Tabasco Province.

Then the girl came to us and offered to show us the cult of the Jaguar God as it still was practiced.

"Impossible!" I snorted, when Jaime, our interpreter, told me of what she had said.

"This is what she tells me, *señor,*" Jaime repeated, shrugging as if to tell me that he wasn't going to worry about problems of possibility or impossibility.

"Bring the girl here," I ordered.

He returned a few minutes later. The girl, who had wandered into our camp half an hour before, had the rare coltish beauty that is sometimes found in isolated pockets of Mexican Indian civilization. I suppose she had the pure blood of the Aztecs in her veins. She was tall, with animated black eyes and

short-cropped black hair; her high cheekbones and thin nostrils gave her a vibrant, vigorous appearance. She wore only a wraparound of some thin fabric that covered her from her breasts to mid-thigh. The expanse of revealed skin was exciting; the skimpy garment plainly revealed the lush contours of her body. I could see the dark-brown nipples jutting through the white cloth, like upthrusting little grapes set on the spheres of her rounded breasts. She had the natural beauty of a jungle fawn.

She poured out a voluble flow of words in an Indian dialect I did not understand.

"What's she saying?" I asked Jaime.

"She says that ten miles from here her people still worship the Jaguar God. That there are temples and statues above ground that don't need to be dug up. She says that if you give her six hundred pesos she will take you to the village."

I whistled. Six hundred pesos is only $50, but even that much is a fortune for an Indian girl. "What does she want that much money for?"

Jaime asked her and got a long reply. Turning to me, he said, "Her

(Continued on next page)

lover has gone to Mexico City. She needs the cash if she wants to follow him."

I nodded, smiling. "All right," I said. "Tell her that it's too late to begin today, but first thing in the morning we'll start out for her village, and if she's telling the truth she'll have her six hundred pesos."

But the Indian girl—Anita, her name was—didn't trust us. "She wants the money *before* we leave."

"Tell her she can have two hundred pesos tomorrow morning, the rest when we get there," I said. "That's the best offer I'll make. She can take it or leave it."

She took it. Through Jaime, I arranged that she would lead us to the village after breakfast the next day. Then I went back to digging.

I knew that if the Indian girl were telling the truth, we were on the threshold of one of the most exciting anthropological finds of the decade. But I knew better than to put much faith in her story. I was willing to risk a few hundred pesos and some boot-leather to find out, because it was foolish to snub the off-chance that she might just be playing it straight with us. But I wasn't counting on finding anything.

There were eighteen members of our group—twelve Mexican laborers and a staff of six, which included a Mexican archaeologist, Dr. Felipe Manuelas; two graduate students from the University of California, Don Buckley and Robert Sanderson; Jaime Morelas, our camp superintendent and interpreter; Norman Rickhardt, our photographer; and, as director of the expedition, myself. It was the first time I had been in charge of a major archeological expedition, and I was anxious to turn in a good job.

The La Venta area has been under exploration since 1940, when a Smithsonian team first dug up the huge stone heads of the Jaguar God. Successive expeditions had uncovered elaborate tombs and monuments of basalt rock and green serpentine in the rain forest along the coastal plain rimming the Gulf of Mexico. They had found more of the 20-ton stone heads of the Jaguar God, and had located great pavementlike mosaic masks and offerings of priceless jade.

We knew that the Olmecs had ruled this part of Mexico as long ago as 291 B.C., and had begun to build their La Venta site about four hundred years after that. We archaeologists believe that the Olmecs may have been the first Central Americans to create a true civilization. They had mathematics, a system of hieroglyphics, and a calendar. They had engineers good enough to know how to move single stones weighing up to 30 tons a distance of 60 miles.

Our expedition had concentrated on digging deep into the La Venta territory, hunting for time-buried relics. In the five years since the previous expedition to the place, the jungle had sprung up fiercely, so much of our work involved mere clearing away.

The girl wandered around our diggings the rest of the day, evidently curious. I couldn't help wondering how much truth there might be in her story. The jungle is pretty rugged in parts of southern Mexico, and it was perfectly possible that there were some undiscovered ruins still being used by the natives. Lord knows there had been enough rumors to that effect.

We knocked off work when it started getting dark, and after eating we went to our cabins. As expedition leader, I had a private room, thatched with palm roofing. The others doubled up, while the laborers slept dormitory-fashion in a longhouse they had constructed.

I had forgotten completely about the girl. I hadn't expected her to go all the way back to her village after dark, but I just didn't figure she would stay around the excavation area either. So I was surprised when she interrupted me at my nightly chore of note-taking. She walked into my cabin without knocking, smiled brightly, and said something in her own language.

I replied, "I didn't know you were still here."

But she understood no Spanish, and I none of her tongue. It was late, nearly midnight. Just about everyone was asleep. And in a sudden quick motion she slipped out of her one-piece garment and threw herself down on my bed.

Her body was a poem in flesh, all soft curves and languorous planes. I didn't know what to do—she wouldn't leave, and she would not or could not understand what I was telling her.

Finally I gave up. I blew out the lamp, took off my shirt and trousers, and lay down on the floor, curling up on a straw mat near the bed.

Instantly she was off the bed. Her warm body nestled against mine. Her fingers agilely peeled away my clothing. I told myself that it was madness to sleep with a native girl, that I might get disease, that I was civilized and should not take advantage of her—

Take advantage? I never had a chance. She took advantage of me. Her fingers wandered over my body, weaving a spell of desire, and finally I could no longer resist. I rose, picking her up with me, and we entwined on the bed. She made love like a creature of nature—with utter abandon. I fell asleep cupping her warm satin-skinned breasts.

Just before I drowsed off, I made a mental note to wake up early and get her out of here before the others found out about it. But sleep gripped me tightly. I heard loud pounding on my door—"Come on, Mal, everybody else is up!" It was Norman Rickhardt's voice. Before I could do anything, Anita leaped from the bed, sprang to the door—a nude brown-skinned nymph—opened it, and gaily chattered in Rickhardt's astonished face.

Nobody said anything about the incident when I came to the break-

I EARN BIG PAY and I WORK EVERY DAY!

AMERICA IS SHORT 100,000 MECHANICS AND 25,000 SHOPS

Train at Home for a Better Job in
AUTOMOTIVE MECHANICS

There's a bright future just ahead for you. The auto industry is short 100,000 mechanics. It also needs 25,000 new repair shops. You can enjoy steady work, high wages—or even a business of your own—*if you are a trained man.* Don't let the "if" stand in your way! It's *easy* to get training.

CTI has a fine, new Home Study course that is very practical, up-to-date and easy to understand. It includes tools and instruments. Before you know it, you'll be working on your own auto, then on other cars—for pay. Perhaps in the local garage, while still a student. *Get more information* on these wonderful job opportunities in America's No. 1 industry. *Mail coupon today.* We'll send our new catalog.

YOU PRACTICE — *YOU GET EXPERIENCE* — USING ENGINE TUNE-UP KIT AND TOOLS

YOU DO NOT PAY EXTRA FOR THESE FINE KITS

No extra charge for tools and tune-up kit. All are yours to use and keep.

Many CTI Students Make Money Soon After They Start Training

CTI trains you to become an all-around mechanic. You learn tune-up and overhaul; electric, cooling and lubricating systems; power steering and brakes; automatic transmissions; etc. Many students, however, start fixing cars soon after they enroll. They work part time "on their own", or in local shops. They add to their incomes, earn enough to pay tuition, and buy shop equipment. Some have a brisk business under way by graduation time. *Our catalog gives you information on how to earn as you learn.*

CTI tools and instruments are professional in design and quality—the kind that experienced mechanics use to do good work faster. You get all necessary mechanic's tools, including socket set, and a tune-up kit which includes: Compression Tester; Vacuum Gauge & Fuel Pump Tester; Ignition Timing Light; and portable, steel case. Using tools and instruments gives you confidence, makes you proud of your craft, speeds up training, and best of all, lets you *learn by practicing.* Yes, you acquire *experience* as you train. No need to spend years as a low-pay apprentice! You practically get on-the-job training in your own home.

FIRST GET THE FACTS—THEN DECIDE
Mail Coupon Today for 2 Free Booklets

DIESEL MECHANICS OR BODY-FENDER REBUILDING instruction is included with your training—at no extra cost. Only Commercial Trades Institute gives you this added choice.

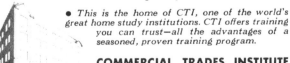

● *This is the home of CTI, one of the world's great home study institutions. CTI offers training you can trust—all the advantages of a seasoned, proven training program.*

COMMERCIAL TRADES INSTITUTE
CHICAGO 26, ILLINOIS

COMMERCIAL TRADES INSTITUTE

1400 GREENLEAF AVENUE DEPT. A 987
CHICAGO 26, ILLINOIS

Mail me your two opportunity booklets: *Make Big Money in Auto Mechanics;* and *Sample Lesson.* Both are FREE.

Name_____ Age_____

Address_____

City_____ Zone____ State_____

fast table twenty minutes later. But I knew that everyone in camp was aware that I had slept with Anita. I sensed a distinct coldness at the table, as though they felt I had lowered myself by being lecherous enough to take an Indian girl into my bed. I didn't try to explain the circumstances; that would only have made things worse. And I knew that beneath their high moral indignation was simple jealousy. From the way they all stole glances at Anita, I knew that there wasn't a man among them who wouldn't have been glad to share his bed with her last night.

To cover my embarrassment I organized the expedition to Anita's village. I decided that the only ones to go would be myself, Jaime, and Rickhardt. I needed a photographer and an interpreter; the other archeologists could come later, if there was anything to see. In the meanwhile they could continue the digging here while I went off to investigate Anita's claim.

The four of us left about half past nine. The sun was not yet high, but it was warm already. There was no use taking the jeep, since the jungle path would not be wide enough.

Anita led us silently along a narrow path lined with tangled vines. Howler monkeys babbled raucously in the treetops, while colorful birds fluttered over our heads, and we kept a careful eye peeled for such dangerous serpents as the rattler, the coral snake, and the fer-de-lance, all of them known to infest this area.

Either Jaime had misunderstood or else Anita had misinformed us, because the village was closer to eighteen miles from our camp than ten. She skipped ahead of us, maintaining a killing pace, and we did our best to keep up with it as the sun rose. But even at forced-march speeds, we couldn't cover more than three or four miles an hour. It was well into the afternoon before we burst through a thick stand of trees and Anita pointed ahead.

"She says the village is right down below," Jaime translated. "She wants her other four hundred pesos now."

"First we see the monuments," I replied stubbornly.

Jaime told her. She replied, and I got the translated gist. "She says all right, but be very careful. Her people don't like contact with *norteamericanos* and they might get violent if they see you."

We edged forward until we had a good view of the village square. It looked like almost any other Indian village in the Mexican jungle, at first glance.

But there was one big exception.

A twenty-foot-high exception.

A statue of the Jaguar God stood smack in the middle of the village square. It was the typical form, just the head, not the body. The harsh, cruel features had been softened and rounded by century after century of exposure to the jungle elements, but this was unmistakably one of the old Olmec idols.

Surrounding it were a horde of smaller images—complete statues of the Jaguar God, about two feet high. We had found many such figurines in our digs, all of them worn and mutilated. But these looked brand new! I began to tingle. Obviously in this isolated pocket of the forest a tribe cut off from time continued the old Olmec ways—including the making of new sacred statues.

I could picture the sensation this story would make in archeological circles. Silently, I handed Anita's remaining pesos over to her. She grinned and thrust the crumpled paper bills into the valley between her high breasts— the breasts I had fondled the night before, I reminded myself guiltily.

"Let's go," I said impulsively. "We've got to talk to these natives—tell them we just want to photograph their statues—"

Anita chattered something.

Jaime said, "She says you mustn't leave hiding."

"Tell her we're not afraid. That we'll take the responsibility in case anything happens."

And without further discussion I stepped boldly out of hiding and into the village square. The others followed me, Anita still talking.

The site was breathtaking. The entire square was paved with polished blocks of green serpentine, forming the familiar features of the Jaguar mask. The square was ornamented with nine gleaming concave mirrors of black metallic hematite, set in a large circle to catch the rays of the sun at different times of the day. It was about the way an Olmec village of the year 300 must have looked.

While Jaime, Rickhardt and I stood in open-mouthed wonder, Anita gave a little scream—and, suddenly, her tribesmen came running up from all sides. We were armed with pistols, but we had no chance even to draw them. Our hands were pinioned behind our backs, lashed with sturdy hemp rope that cut deeply into our wrists.

An old man, ninety perhaps, tottered out. He pointed angrily at the quivering Anita and shouted a stream of unintelligible abuse.

"What's he saying?" I whispered to Jaime.

"He's cursing her for having brought white men to the village. Seems there were some white men here before, and—hold on, let me listen."

By pieces and bits, over the next fifteen minutes, Jaime got the story and relayed it to me. Put all together, it went something like this:

Two white men, hunters perhaps, or soldiers-of-fortune, had wandered into the area several months before. They spoke the Indian dialect well enough to get themselves into the good graces of the villagers, and they had established themselves as residents. Anita had fallen for one of them, and had been visiting his bed every night. This didn't upset the villagers too much, because they were far from puritan, but what *did* get them sore was that in the middle of one night the two white men vanished with as much jade as they could carry. Naturally, this thievery changed the villagers' ideas about white men.

Anita had then announced that she was going to Mexico City to marry one of the white men. For this, she was soundly trounced, and told that if she ever had anything to do with white men again, she would suffer.

But then she had found out that archaeologists were in the neighborhood, and she was smart enough to know that archeologists would pay enough for a peep at her village to cover her fare from Tabasco to Mexico City. So she had made her offer to us, and we had taken her up on it. But she hadn't expected us to step right out in the open the way we had.

If Anita had told us the whole story, maybe we would have been more careful. But she had played us phony, and now we were all in trouble for it.

"What's she saying?" I asked.

"She's pleading for them to let us go. They want to sacrifice us, or something. She says no, just sacrifice her."

Rickhardt and I watched and listened, sweating, wondering how the debate was going. It reached its culmination finally. Two burly tribesmen dragged Anita forth.

"She's going to be the Bride of the Jaguar God," Jaime whispered, and his voice shook.

Methodically Anita's clothes were ripped from her. The folded wad of bills tumbled unnoticed to the ground. They dragged her, squirming, toward the massive stone face of the Jaguar God.

They roped her to the face of the statue, anchoring her wrist-ropes behind the god's ears and tying the ankle-ropes to projections at the corners of its mouth. Then, as she lay spread-eagled across the idol, the old priest approached, a glittering blade in his hand.

I tried to look away, but my eyes kept coming back, of their own accord, to the scene. He calmly carved that magnificent animal body.

He made an incision in each wrist. He sliced through the skin below her breasts. He nipped the thick arteries in her groin. He sawed a slash in her abdomen. Holding her away from the stone face for a moment, he opened veins in her buttocks.

The girl writhed in horrible torment, muscles standing out with clarity on her sleek hide, as blood spouted from a dozen cuts, pouring down over her, staining the face of the idol, pattering onto the mosaic beneath her. As her life began to ebb her head lolled, her skin grew pale beneath its outer coloring.

"The Jaguar God is drinking her blood," Jaime murmured.

We were forced to watch Anita die. I was expecting that we would be next, but, instead, the guards released us. Anita had interceded for us, we were told. We were not to die. But if we ever returned to the village, we would meet a fate ten times as terrible as that handed out to Anita.

Our pistols were taken from us, our bonds were severed, and we were allowed to go stumbling homeward through the gathering darkness. We reached the camp in the small hours of the morning. The others were waiting up, around the fire, worried about us. We told them it had been a hoax, that there had been no Olmec ruins.

But, of course, it was no hoax. The vivid memory of a young girl wrenched with pain testifies to that. Somewhere in the jungles of southern Mexico is a village where old Olmec ways still prevail, where fierce human sacrifice is practiced, where relics of yesteryear are still in current use. I could make my archeological reputation if I ever went back to find that village again. But I never shall.

The end

NUDIST PARADISE ON THE FRENCH RIVIERA

THE DAY after I arrived at the Ile du Levant, on the French Riviera, I was treated to one of the high spots of the entire season—the election of "Miss Ile du Levant" of 1958. The Ile du Levant happens to be my personal nomination for the sexiest place on earth, and the scene that day is proof positive: 2300 naked and near-naked human beings were crammed into a natural amphitheatre to choose a beauty queen from among fifteen absolutely bare belles.

The contest is held each year during the second week of August, at Rioufrede, a pebble beach surrounded by pine slopes, on the shore of this fabulous island. I arrived early, accompanied by Josephine, the 19-year-old Parisian girl who had been my companion since

our arrival the day before. Josephine had had no chance to enroll in the contest, but as far as I was concerned she belonged on the platform. She sat next to me in the hot sun wearing only the so-called *"minimum,"* a minuscule triangle of cloth that covers the loins. Her young, ripe, Bardot-esque body was bare to the sun except for this tiny strip of cloth. I was clad equally skimpily. All about us, though, waiting for the contest to begin, were men, women, and children wearing le *minimum* or less. A girl of about fourteen, her body just beginning to ripen, stood nearby, completely unclad. Flanking her on either side stood her parents, equally nude—a handsome couple in their mid thirties. Her mother, a blonde beauty

with the rounded upthrust breasts of a girl half her age, held a five-year-old boy by the hand, and Junior wasn't wearing anything either.

That was the scene wherever I looked—flesh, flesh, flesh, all of it tanned, most of it bare, much of it sensationally attractive. For the Ile du Levant, just off the south coast of France, is a fashionable public nudist colony that attracts tourists, sightseers,

(Continued on page 50)

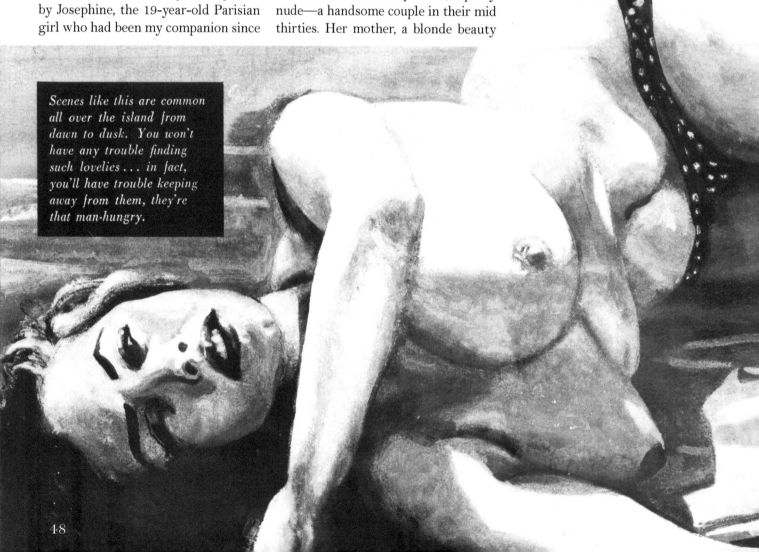

Scenes like this are common all over the island from dawn to dusk. You won't have any trouble finding such lovelies ... in fact, you'll have trouble keeping away from them, they're that man-hungry.

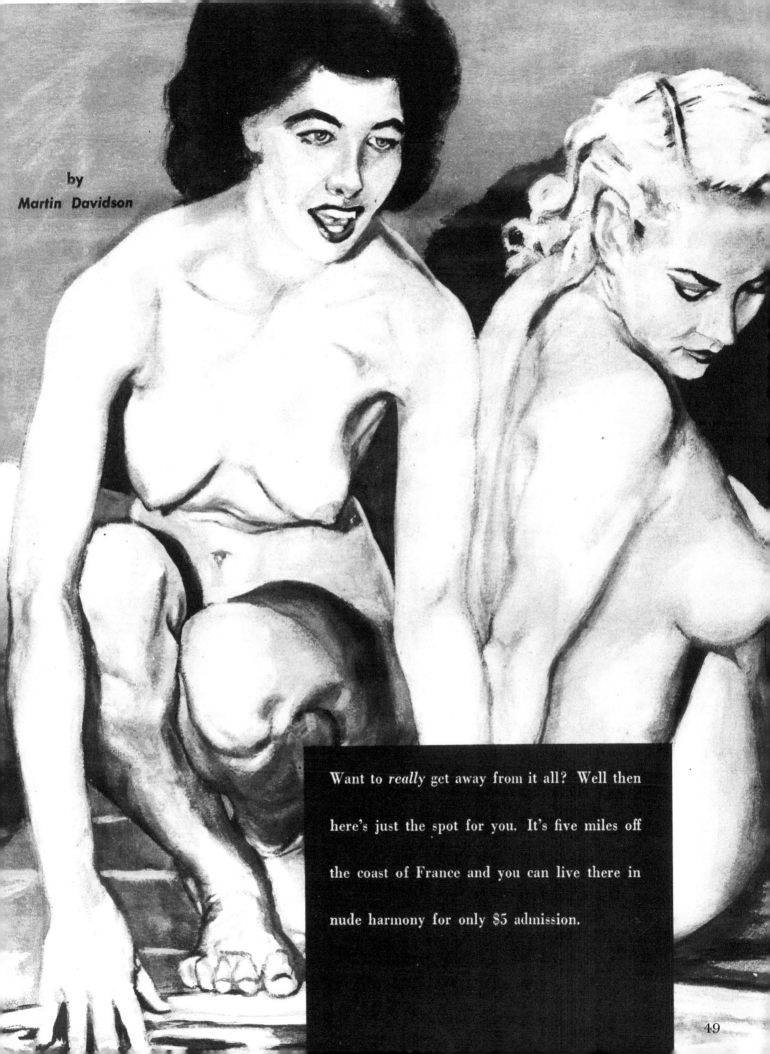

by
Martin Davidson

Want to *really* get away from it all? Well then here's just the spot for you. It's five miles off the coast of France and you can live there in nude harmony for only $5 admission.

49

millionaires, theatrical people, from all over Europe. The world's shapeliest bodies are to be seen here, on free display.

The signal was given for the beginning of the contest. The fifteen girls, deeply tanned and wearing not a stitch, walked slowly up a ramp along the water's edge. To my goggling eyes, each one looked lovelier than the last. As they reached the judging stand, they paused, stretched voluptuously, displaying their beauties of breasts and hips and buttocks, turned slowly, and moved on. At my left, an owlish Roman playwright named Cesare gave me a whispered commentary on each girl.

The first was, according to Cesare, a Belgian girl named Lise—with raven hair, skin tanned deep brown, and ruby-tipped breasts of breathtaking size and perfection. Her place was taken by a Swede, Ragnar, "only sixteen," Cesare murmured—whose abundant blonde glory brought an appreciative cry from the onlookers. Next came a French girl, and a stunner—"Annette, 40–23–38," whispered Cesare. She pirouetted past the judges and drew whistles from the crowd. The rest of the girls passed rapidly before my eyes—a Spanish girl, a damsel from the Netherlands, a London lass, and on, and on, until I had just about lost my capacity to appreciate woman flesh. The judging took nearly twenty minutes, and was marked by evident vigorous disagreements on the platform. Finally the M.C., a distinguished-looking and utterly naked Frenchman, declared the Belgian, Lise, as victor, with all the other girls listed as tied for second place.

"Come," Cesare said. "Let's get out of here before the rioting starts."

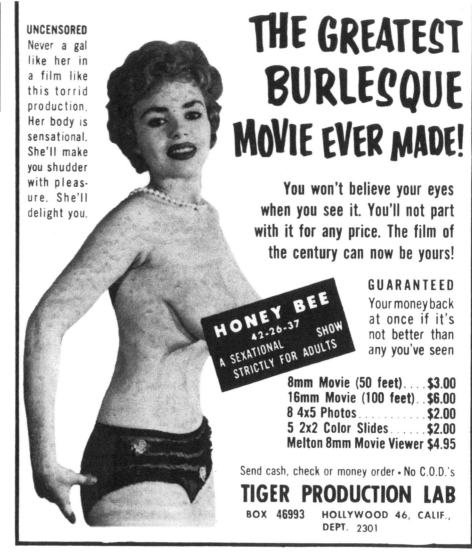

And so the three of us, Cesare, Josephine, and I, beat a hasty retreat. Cesare had judged the situation shrewdly. Fists had already begun to fly as partisans of the various contestants began to let their displeasure with the verdict be known. The riot is an almost invariable sequel to the contest. Looking back, I saw the amphitheater milling with naked forms, while burly lifeguards sent by the proprietor did their best to stem the fighting.

By evening, I was sipping *pernod* in an island bar, Josephine by my side—both of us still wearing only *le minimum*. And later that night we went to bed together for the second time—not bad going, considering we had only known each other two days!

Paradise on Earth? A modern Eden? The Ile du Levant is certainly that. And if the goings-on sound unbe-lievable to you, I sympathize. I couldn't believe in advance, either, when a Parisian friend of mine told me about the Ile du Levant last summer—so I went there to see for myself. If you have the necessary lucre, you might try doing the same. You won't be disappointed, believe me.

The nudist facet of the Ile dates only from 1931, when thirteen disciples of the French naturist Dr. Gaston Durville bought the island and set up a colony there. Before that, it had been a naval base as far back as Roman times.

At my friend's advice, I took the Train Bleu from Paris—a sleeper that arrived in Toulon at 7 AM the following morning. Aboard the train I had noticed a pretty black-haired black-eyed Parisienne travelling alone. It was Josephine, though I didn't know it then. Nor did I know she was heading for the same destination I was.

I breakfasted in the station restaurant at Toulon and then caught the bus to the Riviera harbor of Le Lavandou. Josephine was aboard the bus too. Recognizing me, she smiled shyly.

At Le Lavandou, we were met by the cutter *Lou Cigalou*, owned and operated by Captain Leopold Pagliasco, a barechested piratical looking man who ferries thousands of tourists a year between the mainland and the Ile du Levant at $2 a round trip. Pagliasco also has something of a monopoly on ferrying food to the island, and is a wealthy man as a result.

The ride took almost an hour. The island hove into view finally. The Ile du Levant is two miles wide, ten long, and rises 500 feet above the sea. The shoreline consists of rocky cliffs topped with pine and eucalyptus, and at the very top of the island is Heliopolis, the City of the Sun, heart of the nudist colony. The scenery was overwhelmingly beautiful, we all agreed. By this time Josephine and I had struck up a conversation. She was nineteen, worked as a Parisian model, and was taking a week at the Ile du Levant to get away from it all. "I would *love* to have an affair with an Americain!" she laughed, and I quietly promised myself I would fulfill her wishes.

As the motor cutter pulled in at the Ayguade, which is what the Ile's port is called, a sight even more stupefying than the scenery greeted the newcomers. A crowd of about fifty sunbathers waited on shore to welcome us. Some wore "*le minimum*," others nothing. They shouted gay greetings at us in half a dozen languages. It was bedazzling to take in so much nude flesh in one glance—but this was only the beginning.

The new arrivals were loaded aboard trucks and taken up to Heliopolis. It was a suspense-filled trip along the damnest set of hairpin curves I remember, but we survived it somehow.

We were unloaded in a village square where some yokels were playing a game of what looked like ninepins. We knew they were locals, because they had clothes on. The only people who wear clothes in Heliopolis are the permanent inhabitants, 170 of them, nearly all ex-gangsters from Marseilles who have come out here to run the shops and hotels. The nudist colony, incidentally, takes up only about ten percent of the island. The rest, fenced off, is still property of the French Navy, which has a considerable problem keeping its men from spending all their time gawking at the tourists.

Around the square stood a school, a bakery, a post office, three groceries, four restaurants, and five hotels, the latter being mediocre affairs without running water or electricity. The elite of Heliopolis, people like Françoise Sagan, Orson Welles, Porfirio Rubirosa, Marlene Dietrich, and Errol Flynn, live in yachts off the shore or else stay in costly villas on the hillsides. But the ordinary garden-variety tourists live in the hotels.

Josephine suggested that we cut expenses by sharing a room. I certainly wasn't going to object to that arrangement, so we registered in a room with double bed for the equivalent of $7.50 a day, breakfast included. We registered under our own names, Mr. Martin Davidson and *Miss* Josephine B_____, without getting a rise out of the blasé clerk.

We unpacked quickly, and I suggested a swim. Josephine was agreeable. Modestly turning my back, I stripped and donned the tiny "*minimum*." Glancing around, I saw Josephine totally nude. She made mock gestures of embarrassment, and comically insisted that I close my eyes until she, too, was demurely attired in the scant few square inches of her "*minimum*." Her softly rounded body was a joy to the eye. Hand in hand, we romped down to the beach. I was a little uneasy for the first few seconds, but any embarrassment quickly vanished at the sight of more than a thousand sunbathers toasting themselves in the nude on the beach. It was just like Coney Island, in a way—there were family groups sitting together with thermos bottles and soda pop, little toddlers crawling all over, teenagers playing catch—but everyone was in the nude.

We swam a while, sunbathed a while, and then, as the day reached its end, we returned to our hotel. We dressed in shorts, Josephine donned a halter, and we went out for cocktails and dinner. A bulletin board in the square contained some typical Ile du Levant announcements: "TONIGHT: Ball in Hotel Bellevue...please come without brassieres... Next Sunday at 10 AM: Footrace between Vegetarians and Meat-Eaters ... Annual Meeting of British sunbathers will take place Tuesday in Tent No. 28." And so on.

In the evening there was dancing and drinking, and then early to bed. Josephine melted into my arms. Her skin, warmed by a full afternoon of sunbathing, was like silk or satin. In bed she was voluptuous, abandoned—just the way a healthy French girl of nineteen ought to be. She was thoroughly experienced, too. All in all it was a delightful night, though I got hardly any sleep.

We were out bright and early the next morning, which is when we met the Italian playwright Cesare. He told us about the beauty contest, and also gave me plenty of information about life in this nudist paradise.

For one thing, there's a serpent in Eden. Because most of the permanent settlers are ex-mobsters, several vendettas are carried on regularly, and sometimes the tourists get caught in the middle. Hardly a week goes by without some visitor getting bopped by accident in an island feud.

There are also some questionable elements—sexual perverts of various kinds who tend to lower the island's tone. Also, peepers who anchor yachts off shore and watch the goings-on through powerful binoculars. And other sharpers try to exploit the

Did you ever ask yourself...

WHY CAN'T I GROW HAIR?

First, let's understand a few facts about hair growth and baldness. Common baldness follows a characteristic pattern. The hair recedes at the temples and there is a gradual loss of hair at the crown of the head. Hair lost in this manner is progressive and, if unchecked, the end result is baldness.

You may have seen ads with "before and after" photographs of men and women enjoying renewed hair growth. These photographs are probably authentic. But the next time you pick up one of these ads observe it carefully. Note that the baldness areas do *not* follow the characteristic pattern of common baldness. Note that the bald spots are not on the crown or at the temples. Instead, they are almost on any other part of the head—the back of the head, the side of the head — places where most people still retain hair after many years of being bald. These people were suffering from a scalp disorder called *alopecia areata*, which means loss of hair in patches. In these cases the hair falls out in clumps practically overnight, and grows back the same way after weeks, months, or years later. Doctors don't know the cause of alopecia areata but believe it results from a nervous disturbance.

At any rate, the chances are 98 to 1 that *you do not have alopecia areata.*

NOW YOU CAN STOP WORRYING ABOUT BALDNESS

Now we can clear the air. Up to this time no one has discovered how to GROW HAIR ON A BALD HEAD. No, nothing known to modern science, no treatment, no electric gadget, no chemical, no brush, no formula can GROW HAIR. So, if you are already bald, make up your mind you are going to stay that way. Quit worrying about it—enjoy yourself.

But if you are beginning to notice that your forehead is getting larger, beginning to no-

tice too much hair on your comb, beginning to be worried about the dryness or oiliness of your hair, the itchiness of your scalp, the ugly dandruff—these are Nature's Red Flags. They warn you that if these conditions go unchecked, baldness may be the end result.

Yes, there *is* something you can do to help save your hair.

The development of the amazing new formula series called Alophene may mean that thousands of men and women can now *increase the life expectancy* of their hair. Alophene has two basic formulas, with the dual purpose of correcting a scalp condition that often results in baldness, and giving greater health and longer life to the hair you still have.

HOW ALOPHENE WORKS ON YOUR SCALP

This is how Alophene works: (1) It tends to normalize the secretions of your sebaceous glands, controlling excessive dryness and oiliness. A few treatments, and your hair looks more beautiful, more vital, and healthier. By its rubifacient action, it stimulates blood circulation to the scalp, thereby supplying more nutrition to the hair follicles. It supplies Vitamin A to the scalp, which some medical authorities believe may be an essential nutritive factor to the hair and scalp.

(2) As an effective antiseptic, Alophene kills, on contact, seborrhea-causing bacteria believed by many medical authorities to be a cause of baldness. By its keratolitic action, it dissolves dried sebum and ugly dandruff, it controls seborrhea, thereby tending to normalize the lubrication of the hair shaft, and eliminating head scales and scalp itch. In short, Alophene offers a modern effective treatment for the preservation of your hair.

Today there is no longer any excuse for any man or woman to neglect the warning signals of im-

pending baldness. After years of research and experimentation, we can say this about Alophene. We know of no other treatment, used at home or in professional salons, that can surpass Alophene in saving your hair.

ALOPHENE IS UNCONDITIONALLY GUARANTEED

Therefore, we offer you this UNCONDITIONAL GUARANTEE. Try Alophene in your own home. In only 10 days your hair must look thicker, more attractive and alive. Your dandruff must be gone, your irritating scalp itch must stop. In only 20 days you must see the remarkable improvement in your scalp condition, and the continued improvement in the appearance of your hair. After 30 days you must be completely satisfied with the rapid progress in the condition of your hair and scalp, or return the unused portion of the treatment and we will refund the entire purchase price at once.

You now have the opportunity to help *increase the life expectancy of your hair*—at no risk.

So don't delay. Nothing — not even Alophene—can grow hair from dead follicles. Fill out the coupon below, while you have this chance to enjoy thicker - stronger - healthier HAIR AGAIN.

©BLYTHE-PENNINGTON, LTD., 23 West 44th St., New York 36, N. Y campers who, not being able to afford the high rates at Heliopolis, camp in the shrubbery above a sandy beach called Les Grottes, paying a daily fee of about four cents for the privilege. Frequently signs will be posted at Les Grottes advertising for pretty models for naturist photographs. Since many of the campers there are poverty-stricken girls who have hitchhiked long distances to reach the Ile, they succumb to these signs, are paid about $1.50 an hour for posing in the nude, and then, sometimes, are compelled forcibly to pose for pornographic films with male models.

The island is frequented by celebrities who drop in incognito for a one-day visit, generally hiding behind dark sunglasses to avoid publicity.

All told, I spent seven days in Heliopolis. My stay there was enlivened by a dramatic production of a French classic play by Racine—with the actors wearing masks and sandals, but nothing in between. Wherever I strolled on the island I saw artists at work, sculpting or painting—and no model fees to pay! There were afternoon dances, too. At these, *"le minimum"* is required, to prevent possible embarrassing sexual stimulation as the dancers cling, body pressed against bare body, and move slowly through their steps.

The island has its own church, built several years ago, and clothing is required there too—not merely *"le minimum,"* either. The parish priest never misses an opportunity to denounce the shameless nudism of the island, but so far he hasn't gotten his message across. It's a common sight to see devout worshippers leave Mass and peel completely to the buff on the very steps of the church—obediently wearing their clothes inside, but stripping the moment they get out.

Plenty of extracurricular entertainment goes on in the lavish hillside villas. We heard of one couple, a Paris lawyer and his wife, both near fifty, which roams the beaches looking for particularly handsome young couples willing to earn an extra thousand francs or so. Three or four such couples perform at the villa every night, putting on an uninhibited sex exhibition for the benefit of a score of wealthy Frenchmen. I tried to wangle an invite to this gathering, but couldn't manage it. I *was* offered a chance to perform, but turned it down.

Plenty of sex, as you can imagine, is available on the island. Many of the tourists simply shack up with each other, as Josephine and I did. Others come in groups of couples, and swap wives merrily. For those who have no luck picking up other tourists, there is local talent in the well-stacked forms of half a dozen waitresses and chambermaids willing to roll in the hay for a reasonable amount of cash.

Because of the number of small children on the island, it isn't considered cricket to make love in public. Therefore there's even less necking and petting on the beaches than you can find at Coney Island, though wonderful things go on after dark. Occasionally, however, the urge becomes uncontrollable, and it's not uncommon to stumble across an intertwined pair loving it up in the shrubbery. One of my most vivid memories of the Ile du Levant is of the time I accidentally came across a boy of twenty and a full-breasted belle of about fifteen engaged in a violent bout of lovemaking on the ground, while an audience of some half-dozen children, ages five to seven, had collected and was watching with evident interest. But such sights are rare on the Ile. Most of the sex is after dark, and there's plenty of it.

I also got the lowdown on some of the residents who spend most of the year on the Ile and are considered "permanents." One of them is a Paris surgeon in his seventies who must have found *Lolita* an interesting book, because his chief delight is luring little girls between 10 and 12 into his garden and giving them a cold shower. There's also an ex-prisoner-of-war from Germany who has convinced a goodly crowd of followers that he is a reincarnation of Buddha. Also present is the Duchess de Ligne, related to the Belgian royal family, who was tried and acquitted of murdering her husband and now spends all year round here, completely nude, fending off trespassers with an immense watchdog. Another local ornament is the postmaster, richest landowner on the island—and, despite this, a passionate Communist.

At the end of the week, Josephine's vacation came to its end, and she made arrangements to return to Paris. I decided to leave Heliopolis at the same time, because I noticed a peculiar psychological effect creeping over me—I was becoming numb to nudity. The sight of a pair of bare breasts no longer made my eyes swivel. Curving hips, provocative buttocks, seductive thighs, had all lost much of their appeal. Only in the evening when clothes reappeared, did I begin to respond to feminine charms again. Psychologists say that this is an inevitable consequence of getting too much of a good thing. An overdose of bare beauty produces sexual indigestion, or something.

And so I left the Ile du Levant and returned to Paris. I kissed Josephine goodbye, chastely, at the station, and never saw her again. For her, as well as for me, the week we spent together was a week out of time, a week in Paradise, where all sins are forgiven and forgotten. Now, returning to civilization, we went our separate ways. Standing in the train station, I eyed the busy Parisians bustling past me, and tried to picture them as they would look on the Ile du Levant. It was hard for me to believe that only a day before I had lived on an island where the conventions of western society simply did not exist.

As soon as I get the chance, I'm going to go back to Heliopolis. One week at a time is all I need—but I can't wait for my next trip to the Riviera, and, brother, I suggest that you look in on the Ile du Levant too. In a world that keeps getting increasingly grimmer every day, it's the closest thing to Paradise there is.

The end

There wasn't much to do during the hot noon hours except take it easy on the smooth beach with a coconut shell full of rum and a lovely native girl at your side.

One of the few outposts of happiness left on this earth is rapidly disappearing under the heavy hand of commercialism. This may well be the last account we shall ever hear of...

TAHITI, LUSTY ISLAND OF UNTAMED WOMEN

By Leonard Colman
As told to Mark Ryan

OFTEN WISH I could go back there, but I know that Tahiti is forever closed to me now. I have nothing left of it but memories—of that climate that's always spring, of the brownskinned, laughing, full-breasted girls who gave themselves to me so willingly, of the long days snoozing on the beaches, sipping the local brew, splashing in the sparkling sea. All gone, now, as far as I'm concerned. Gone, too, are the incredible ceremonies I witnessed in Tahiti's jungled inlands, gone the gay and carefree life. It's all over and done with. The French authorities have put up the barrier, now: No Beachcombers

Wanted. But I was there when the going was good, and, let me tell you, it's the closest I've ever been to Paradise on Earth.

And Paradise was what I was looking for in 1945, too. I had just had four years of hell, U.S. Marine Corps variety. I was smack in the middle of Polynesia when V-J day arrived that summer. I was twenty-six and had nothing to go back to in the States except the dull routine of some job. And I told myself that after four years of ducking Nipponese slugs, I had earned a nice, healthy vacation. So, like many another G.I., I said "No thanks" when the time came for me to be shipped home, and, pocketing my discharge papers, I headed for the beaches of Tahiti.

You can't do that now, you see. The French authorities turn down five or six hundred visa applications a month, now. When you apply, these days, you have to give an acceptable reason for wanting to go to Tahiti—and telling them that you just want to loaf is not considered acceptable. You also have to post a bond with the island authorities as a guarantee against becoming a beachcomber. Tourists can get in for short-term stays, provided they prove that they'll have the wherewithal to get themselves homeward when their visa expires. But the day of the permanent beachcomber is finished— killed by guys like me, I guess.

But I had it good. It was December, 1945, when I hit Tahiti. I didn't have any special plans. None of us did. Even then, the island authorities refused to sell property to outsiders, or even

(Continued on next page)

55

to let settlers go into business. But I didn't worry about that. I had plenty of Uncle Sam's green dollars in my pocket, and in the South Pacific that's the greenest green there is.

I found myself a little cabin in Papeete, which is Tahiti's capital city and contains about half the island population. My cabin was about a block from the beach. Who could ask for anything cushier?

There were about half a dozen Marine buddies of mine in the area, as well as a lot of other beachcombing G.I.s I didn't know. And life was one long picnic for us. The locals were crazy about showing us their gratitude for having saved them from the Jap menace. For the first month it was one party after another, some given by the French settlers, some by the natives.

And the women?

The first was Roraima. She was nineteen, a girl with the soft brown skin and lustrous black hair of the full-blooded Polynesian. I found her waiting for me in my cabin one afternoon, a week after my arrival. I had

been out for a swim with two of my pals, and I came back for a little nap. And there she was, sitting perched on the edge of my bed. She was wearing a *lava-lava*, the flower-decorated cloth garment that's practically a national uniform on Tahiti. She smiled shyly at me.

"Hello," I said, startled. "Who the deuce are you?"

"I am Roraima. You live alone, American?"

"Why—yes," I spluttered.

"I would like to work for you. I will do your cooking, your sewing, your cleaning. You will pay me two dollah a week, yes?"

Frowning, I said, "But I didn't advertise for a girl."

"I saw you yesterday. You were alone. Man should not be alone. Two dollah, I will be your *vahine*."

I hesitated, more because I was still overcoming my surprise than because I didn't like the idea of having Roraima work for me as my girl-of-all-work. But she took my silence for disapproval. She stood up and with a quick motion unwrapped her *lava-lava*. It fell in folds at her feet.

She was nude underneath, and her body was a thing of soft curves and beckoning warmth. Her breasts, full and rounded like melons, swayed with each breath. She turned slowly, letting

me look at her perfect back and the twin brown globes of her buttocks.

"You like now?" she asked.

I nodded. "Yes, Roraima. Yes, I like very much."

"I keep you happy. I show you now."

All I was wearing was a pair of swimming trunks. She had them off me in a minute, and pulled me down onto the mattress.

On Tahiti, a girl begins to have lovers at the age of ten or eleven. By the time she reaches Roraima's age, she's an absolute expert.

So Roraima got the job. As my *vahine*, she kept the cabin in order, mended my clothes when they started to wear thin, fashioned me *lava-lavas* and *pareus* to wear, went to market and haggled with the shopkeepers to save me a dime on my food, and gave me the benefit of her fabulous body every night. All for a salary of two dollah a week.

The months slipped by in a pleasant blur. Even with the low cost of living, my money was gradually running out, and I kept making vague promises to myself about getting a job. But the devilish part of life on Tahiti is that it robs you of all backbone. The sultry heat, the warm beaches, the hot women, the free food that can be plucked off any palm—things like this give you the *mañana* complex. There's always time to worry about that job tomorrow, you keep telling yourself. And tomorrow never comes.

One day, though, I woke up and found that Roraima was gone. She had taken her few belongings from my cabin and vanished.

I asked a Frenchman I had become friendly with if he had seen her. "She didn't steal anything of mine, but she took all her own stuff."

"You had better forget her, Colman."

"Why do you say that?"

"She has gone to live with a native boy at the southern end of the island. I heard her telling my *vahine* about it yesterday."

"You knew she was leaving? And you didn't tell me?"

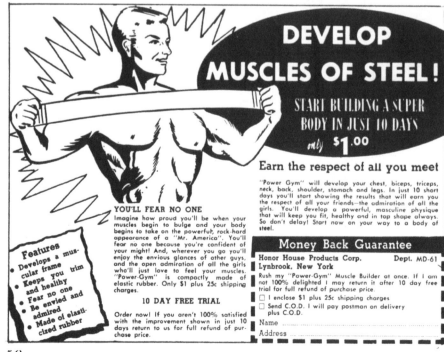

"What good would that have done?" he asked. "A Tahitian comes and goes as she pleases. You could not have stopped her from leaving."

I turned away, bitter and upset. I had thought I was in love with Roraima, and she with me. But I couldn't have been wronger. She liked me, sure—everyone on Tahiti likes everybody else. And maybe she pitied me because I was alone, those first few days. But she didn't intend to spend the rest of her life with me. She had run off with a Tahitian boyfriend, and that was that. Probably she had forgotten I existed by now.

At that time I was still a newcomer, and didn't understand Tahitian ways. Everything is casual there, including romance. The Tahitians dislike the idea of permanent marriage more than any of the other innovations the European settlers have brought. They just don't see why a man should tie himself up with a woman, or a woman with a man, for a permanent span of time. The way they figure it, all love dies sooner or later, and when love is gone from a marriage the sensible thing is for the partners to go their separate ways and fall in love with new mates. Similarly, they have no objections to what we would call adultery. Even when a Tahitian couple is living together, nobody makes a fuss if the lass decides to spend an occasional night under another roof. In our part of the world, such beliefs would cause complete chaos, but somehow the system works on Tahiti.

So Roraima had decided she had had about enough of me, and had picked up and moved on. In my Western way, I was hurt—but not for long. Before the week was out, I had myself a new *vahine*.

I must have had fifteen or sixteen mistresses in my five-year stay on Tahiti. And I got to like the system. Just about the time my gal and I got tired of each other, we would split up, and along would come another. Some of the girls were neat, some sloppy; some cooked well, some badly. But they were all beautiful. They all

had the firm, handsome breasts that Polynesian women—who don't cramp their uppers into rubber-lined contraptions—have. They all were splendid bedmates.

Somewhere in the middle of my second year, the last of my savings ran out. For a week or so I lived on what amounted to charity, and then I got a job on a fishing boat for two weeks. The pay wasn't much, but it would keep me in booze and food for two weeks more. For the rest of my stay on Tahiti, that was my pattern: two weeks of work, then two weeks of living off my earnings until the money ran out.

By 1948, a lot of my G.I. buddies were gone, either to other islands or back to the States. But there were still plenty of us here, roaming the beaches, getting a little bored with life in the Garden of Eden but lacking both the cash and the initiative to go elsewhere.

I got a kick out of watching the newcomers arrive. Every time a freighter came through, it took three times as long for it to unload and load as at any other port. An eighteen-hour job dragged out to four days in Tahiti's sleepy climate, and then it took three days more to round up the crew and separate them from the native women!

I discovered that there was a lot of dope addiction on Tahiti. Thank God, that was one thing I kept away from. But Papeete is full of opium smokers who were introduced to the habit by pushers operating out of China. The Chinese Reds have done a lot to cut down on the opium trade, but when I was there Chiang Kai-Shek's boys still had the upper hand, and the trade thrived. You can see the addicts nonchalantly wandering around Papeete with the small black opium pipes in their mouths. Addicts also hold most of the jobs in Tahiti, since they're the only ones who need money. They work as waiters and hotel porters, clerks and delivery boys, dock hands and government flunkies. The only job they don't take is housework. Nobody will hire an addict when he can have a soft young damsel as his *vahine*.

The one part of Tahitian life you

don't hear much about is the native religion. It isn't quite voodoo, but it's a close relation. The rituals are presided over by witch doctors who have enormous influence on the island, even among natives who are seven-eighths "civilized." If a witch doctor puts a hex on you, a native will tell you, you will die. A witch doctor can strike you with sterility, or he can make a barren woman conceive. A witch doctor can give you syphilis if he mumbles the right words in your direction. Or so you'll be told.

Early in 1949 my current *vahine*, a black-eyed lovely named Haraua, invited me to go up into the jungle hill country with her and witness a tribal ceremony. I didn't have any objections, so we set out together. No sooner were we out of Papeete than Haraua stripped off the upper half of her garments. The missionaries have been working hard to develop a sense of modesty in the natives, but I'm glad to say they've succeeded only in Papeete. Outside of town the old ways still hold true.

Haraua had the most magnificent breasts I had ever seen, in the bargain. They looked like balloons bobbing on her chest, but there was nothing grotesque or flabby about them. They were just big.

She led me upcountry to the site of the celebration. The witchdoctor was a little dubious about having me there, but in typical easygoing local fashion said that it was all right for me to watch, provided I didn't take any photographs. Since I didn't own a camera, it was easy to agree to that.

It was a three-day blowout. The central feature of the outdoor temple was a gigantic mass of stone shaped in the form of a male. Fifty Tahitian women danced stark naked around this bizarre idol by the light of flickering fires, while fifty men squatted outside the circle and provided a rhythmic accompaniment of handclaps. The witch doctor chanted during the dance.

Round and round the stone image the girls went. They were fueled up with a native drug made from the palms. It's a thick, milky substance that can kill you if you drink it straight. The Tahitians thin it out with alcohol, and it makes one hell of a potent punch. I was allowed to sample some. They served it in a cup made out of a small coconut shell, containing about a thimbleful, and it felt like I'd had a pint of moonshine.

When the dancing was ended, the women, half drunk, advanced on the men and picked them out at random. Then they made love by the light of the full moon. I had a few Western inhibitions about making love in a crowd, but they vanished under the influence of the sip of palm-juice I had had. I was claimed by a girl who couldn't have been more than fifteen, with narrow hips and small, pointed breasts. She may have had a boyish build, but the way she made love was strictly feminine.

The orgy went on for three days and nights, giving everybody a chance to join up with at least a dozen different partners. Then, exhausted by my efforts, I got Haraua and we went back to Papeete. Some of the shindigs, I understand, last a week or more. The French authorities make sporadic attempts at stamping them out, but it proves impossible.

Shortly after, a scandal developed when a Dutchman in Papeete offered for sale a set of juicy photographs of native rituals. Since that time, no westerners have been allowed up in the hills to watch, so I was lucky enough to sneak in under the wire.

I might have gone on beachcombing forever, I guess. It was a grand life. Easy loving, easy living. As the months passed I slipped more and more into the lackadaisical Tahiti ways. It's an island where no one has a conscience, where only today counts and to hell with worrying about tomorrow.

But then in 1950 the Korean war broke out. I had loafed for five straight years. Now I owed the world some service. So I turned over a new leaf and worked until I had accumulated enough cash to book passage for San Francisco. I figured I would put in a few more years fighting for my country, and then return to Tahiti for another five or ten years of beachcombing.

Go ahead, tell me I was a damn noble idiot. I guess I was. I froze up in Korea for three years, narrowly missing getting my head shot off a couple of times. And then, finally, the war was over, the truce was signed, and I was a civilian again. I felt pretty good about myself. I was looking forward to going back to Tahiti.

But the French had put down the bars.

Beachcombers aren't wanted any more. Entrance restrictions are ten times as tough as they were a few years ago. I stormed and raged and appealed to heaven above, but it got me nowhere. The French officials smiled and shrugged and said, *"Pardonnez moi,* but you may not have a visa, Msieu."

So that's what you get for being a hero, I suppose. I don't regret having volunteered to fight for democracy, but I wish I had some way of getting back into Tahiti. There isn't another island in the world like it. I'm back in the States now, working a forty-hour week, and to see me you'd never think that a decade ago I was a bearded bum on the white beaches of Papeete. But that's the way the ball bounces, I guess. At least I had my five years in Paradise while the going was good. And though I've had my share of loving here, it isn't the same at all. I keep longing for the feel of honey-brown Polynesian breasts. I keep remembering Roraima's shy smile that first day as she sent her *lava-lava* tumbling to the floor. I remember that fantastic three days in the hills. And I envy the lucky bastards who are still there, drifting in that sky-blue ocean.

But, in a way, I'm glad I've escaped the call of Tahiti. It's Paradise on Earth, true enough. A man gets everything he wants. But it's easy to be pulled under. Maybe I'm better off here, working for my living like all the rest of you. I don't know. I guess I never will. But it was wonderful while it lasted.

The end

Ride in Air Conditioned Comfort on Hottest Days

Only $9⁹⁵

- New scientific portable construction.
- Liquid fuel cooling agent.
- Cools your car in seconds.
- Racy, modernistic design.

Jet-Air
Filters, Washes and Cools the Air in Your Car

This interior view of "Jet Air" shows how the special air flow filter breathes in atmospheric air and blows it into the compressing chamber. There, it is trapped in the liquid fuel cooling chamber and the temperature is dropped enormously. Then, this conditioned air is slowly released into the car creating a refreshing cool and interior temperature that is continuous and pure.

LABORATORY TESTS PROVE

Conclusive laboratory TESTS prove "Jet Air's" efficiency. Under strict laboratory conditions, we raised the temperature of a 1957 Bel Air Chevrolet to a hot, muggy 111° Fahrenheit. We then installed "Jet Air". Instantly cool refreshing air entered the car, and within 90 seconds, the temperature had dropped 34° and was still going down. We were cool, comfortable and refreshed. Within 6 minutes, the temperature was 67° .. a total drop of 44°.

RIDE IN SAME COMFORT AS IN EXPENSIVE AIR CONDITIONED CARS

"Jet Air" gives you cool refreshing air that makes your car Degrees Cooler in Seconds on even the hottest days. Just think what this means to you. It means that the hottest day of the summer, the streaming roads of traffic congested highways, the short tedious shopping trips, etc., now all become joyous means of escaping the heat. Yes, while other drivers are sitting and suffering, you are cooler, more comfortable and content. Yes, with "Jet Air" we guarantee that you must feel as comfortable as in expensive air conditoning or it doesn't cost you a cent!

WORKS ON SAME PRINCIPLE AS RAM JET ENGINE

"Jet Air" works on the same scientific principle as a Ram Jet. Equipped with a special "air flow" filter, it inhales the atmospheric air and compresses it in the frost chamber. Then, the air is slowly trapped in the liquid fuel cooling chamber, where the air is released in a refreshing, steady, cool breeze into the car interiors, thus giving you and all your passengers a "spring" ride even on the hottest summer days.

SWEPT WING DESIGN WORKS FUNCTIONALLY — ADDS BEAUTY

Portable and constructed of special lightweight polyethylene to insure maximum refrigeration.

"Jet Air" fits right between the window and the roof of your car. Pregrooved and completely adjustable to any size window, it will not obstruct the view of the driver in any way. And, the sleek "Swept Wing" design which is functionally geared for maximum cooling, adds a racy, modernistic design. Even the most "hard to please" buyers find that "Jet Air" enhances their cars' design and beauty, and "Jet Air" attracts the admiring attention of all other motorists. "Jet Air" is completely portable, & can be installed and removed in less than one minute without any tools or mechanic necessary. Because of its unique construction and sealed cooling unit, we unconditionally guarantee "Jet Air" against mechanical defects or malfunction at any time.

NEW MATERIALS INSURE LIFETIME USE

"Jet Air's" unique construction and special liquid fuel cooling agent insure lifetime use. Yes, we guarantee that you will enjoy the beneficial comforts of "Jet Air" each and every hot day for the life of your present auto, or we will refund your money. Attach in a jiffy, close all the car windows and relax in cool comfort. Only $9.95 complete. Nothing else to buy—No other charges. So don't delay. Order now in time for complete summer comfort. If you are not 100% thrilled and delighted, then simply return for prompt refund of full purchase price.

MONEY BACK GUARANTEE

ATT: Dealers:

For dealer inquiries, kindly address all correspondence on your company stationery to Jet-Air Co. Sales Management Division, Lynbrook, New York. All response will be treated as confidential.

LIFETIME GUARANTEE

"Jet Air" is unconditionally guaranteed to keep you cool and comfortable in your car throughout the summer months for the lifetime of your present car. We further guarantee that you will incur no additional expense after you purchase "Jet Air"; that "Jet Air" requires no attachments, can be installed and removed in seconds. We also guarantee that "Jet Air" will be such an attractive addition to your car that it will receive enthusiastic comments from all your friends and neighbors.

JET-AIR- CO., Dept. MM-8
LYNBROOK, N.Y.
Rush my Portable "Jet Air" liquid fuel cooling unit at once. If I am not delighted I may return for prompt refund or full purchase price.
( ) I enclose $9.95   Same Guarantee
( ) Send C.O.D. I will pay postman on delivering and shipping charge.

Name

Address

By *David F. Killian*

EGYPT'S CITY OF PROSTITUTES

Even though fatso Farouk is out of the way, the new Egyptian government has done nothing to improve the old quarter of the ancient city known around the world for its filth, violence and women.

I N 1952 the Egyptian army gave fatso King Farouk the heave-ho, and much noise was made by the new bosses, General Naguib and Colonel Nasser, about how fast corruption and vice was going to be abolished in the land of the Nile. But those of us who knew how deeply entrenched in Egyptian life are sin and corruption were politely skeptical. I was among the skeptics.

I had been in Egypt from 1946 through 1948, working for a British import–export house. Last fall, while making a business trip through the troubled Arab world, I was asked by the editor of *Exotic Adventures* to take a look-see through my old haunts in Cairo and report on just how much cleaning up there actually has been.

Egypt wears a new name now, ever since it merged with Syria to form the United Arab Republic. But inside Egypt hardly anyone but the upper-crust educated people seems aware of this change in name. To most, the country is still *"Misr,"* as it's been for thousands of years. And as far as the Egyptian man-in-the-

street is concerned, Farouk might just as well be still on his throne. General Naguib is in enforced retirement, and the country is run by the ambitious, energetic Nasser, who wants to be the George Washington of the Arab world—or maybe the Adolf Hitler. In any event, the only change that's visible in Egypt is on the postage stamps, which now bear the slogans of the U.A.R. instead of Farouk's bloated features. Otherwise, all remains the same. The bribery, the theft, the prostitution, all continue as they did in the days of Haroun al-Raschid.

I had a little difficulty getting my entry visa into Egypt. Ever since the Suez ruckus, Nasser's regime has been very very nasty about issuing visas. You can't get into the United Arab Republic if you're Jewish, for one thing. And even if you're not, you can't enter Egypt if your passport is stamped with an Israeli visa. You see, Egypt doesn't recognize the existence

(Continued on page 62)

He got the story, and it wasn't a pretty one, first hand from one of the women in the city of prostitutes.

of Israel, and okaying a passport that also contained an Israeli official document would amount to recognition.

Knowing this, I had carefully arranged my itinerary so I would not set foot on Israeli territory until after I had visited the Arab countries. And in the blank for "*Religion*" I could write *Protestant* with a clear conscience, even though I haven't been inside a church since my confirmation. But though I was neither Jewish nor had an Israeli visa in my passport, I still had to argue a little before I could get admitted to the United Arab Republic. It's all part of Nasser's policy of showing the West how tough he can get.

But finally I arrived in Cairo for a brief stay. There were a few outward signs of change—some new hotels, most of them built with Russian money, and a bit of repaving on the ancient streets. But the city still had the age-old reek of Arabian depravity.

There was one specific test I wanted to make of the Nasser regime: I wanted to have a look through El Berqa.

The Berqa is the red-light district of Cairo. When I was last in Egypt, I was struck by its appalling corruption, its almost bestial ways of purveying lust. No government really bent on a cleanup job could allow El Berqa to continue untouched, teeming as it was not only with every manner of vice, but with conspiracy, intrigue, and blackmail.

El Berqa as I had known it in 1946–49 was a festering sore spreading through a confined section of Cairo. It was a walled city within the city, which had thrived and fluorished on the money it took from the hordes of Allied troops that had been quartered in Cairo during the war years. Hungry for female companionship, swarms of French, British, Australian, South African, and American troops had availed themselves of the services of El Berqa's women, leaving behind vast sums of money and, more often than not, taking away in exchange a good dose of venereal disease.

Out of sheer curiosity I had gone for a look at El Berqa in 1946. It made an unforgettable impression on me, then, and a comparison in 1958 would be a good way of judging the reforms made by the new rulers of Egypt. So I set out on foot from my hotel to have a look at the Berqa of today.

You enter the Berqa by passing through an ornate arched gateway that gives access to a twisting maze of narrow, cobble-paved old streets. Just inside the gate is a prophylactic station maintained by the Egyptian government for the benefit of customers. It's a pretty filthy-looking prophylactic station, not having improved any in the decade between my visits. It was a bad sign.

The instant I got through the gates I was surrounded by a horde of Egyptian kids wearing soiled nightgown-like *galabeas*. They ranged in age from about seven-and-a-half to sixteen. I had the uncanny sensation of *deja vu*, the feeling that the past was repeating itself. And it was. The boys were different, but exactly the same thing had happened to me the last time I had come through these gates.

They clustered around me. Some of them were horrible to look at— they were victims of trachoma, the

eye disease so common in Egypt, and swarms of tiny black flies clung to the masses of pus oozing from their near-blinded eyes.

"Kwoys bint?" they screamed shrilly. "Want a girl? Nice girl? Clean girl?"

Some of them tugged me one way, some another, and as they fought over me they cried the praises of the girl they were pimping for. "Come see my sister—knockers like this," a nine-year-old cried in colloquial American, illustrating what he meant by bunching his fists at his chest. "No, come with me—my sister fifteen, pretty!" "My sister love you good, Mister!" And they would add an explicit catalogue of the particular perversions their sisters specialized in.

I knew they would give me no peace, so I pulled a handful of coins from my pockets and tossed them into the street. The ragamuffins went scrambling after them, and I darted quickly across the square and turned left into a dark, narrow side street, which looked as sinister as anything in the Arabian Nights' repertoire. I found myself standing outside a small sidewalk cafe, and before I could move on, the proprietor, a fez-wearing Arab as fat as Farouk himself, came scuttling out and pleaded with me to accept his hospitality. "Nice cold tea, Turkish coffee?" he crooned. "Or more fun upstairs? Come—I show." And from the depths of his apron he produced a sheaf of well-thumbed glossy photos, about five by six. Each of them showed a girl in the nude, in some obscene posture. "My girls," he said. "You have any one, just one pound."

The girls were magnificent full-bodied creatures that would have graced a Sultan's harem. It was an old racket—show the pictures as a come-on, collect the fee, usher the victim into one of the upstairs bedrooms, and confront him, not with the girl he had picked from the photo, but with some spavined old wreck of a broad. If he complains, he's wasting his breath. The proprietor will simply say, "Sorry, my Ainglish not so good. I never say you sleep with same girl in photo,

meester." And if you complain further, you may find yourself crumpled up in an alley with a broken skull.

Getting myself loose from the fat Arab's clutches, I ordered a cup of Turkish coffee. The cup was dirty and the coffee looked and tasted like warm mud. I took three sips and moved onward.

I hadn't gone more than half a dozen steps when a thin, wizened Levantine scurried up to me. "You will like this," he said to me in French. He drew a packet of color photos from his pocket and fanned them in front of my face. They showed men and women engaged in activities that can't even be described here. And some of the women were unmistakably westerners, too. He babbled his sales pitch, half in French, half in English. These snapshots had been taken through peepholes in the fancy Cairo hotels, he said. Diplomats, actors and actresses, very important people. Three hundred mils a photo, the whole set of twenty for five Egyptian pounds.

The Egyptian pound being worth about $2, I was being offered a bargain rate. I don't have much interest in owning pornography, but I wanted a couple of these photos as evidence for friends back in the U.S. They were absolutely the filthiest things that could be imagined. I offered the peddler five hundred mils—slightly over fifty cents—for two of the pictures. He accepted greedily, let me pick two, and disappeared almost at once. Only later did I realize why the pictures were being sold so cheaply—he had undoubtedly stolen them a few minutes before from some other dealer, and wanted to unload them in a hurry.

I moved on, and every few feet I was accosted by an enterprising citizen of Nasser's uncorrupted country. Some were *hasheesh*-peddlers, others were pimping for their sisters or wives or daughters, others wanted to sell me banned books or hot photos or even rare and no doubt phony postage stamps.

I walked on through the narrow streets lined with the two- and

three-story stuccoed buildings, and from a doorway to my right I heard a low, erotic voice call, "I can give you some fun, American."

I turned. The girl standing in the doorway was perhaps sixteen or seventeen. Dusky, sultry-eyed, she was clad in a dark robe that concealed the contours of her body. A British gold sovereign dangling on a chain round her neck was her sole ornament. Smiling voluptuously at me, she gently lifted her hand to her throat and with a languid motion of arm and shoulder caused her robe to fall open just enough to reveal to me the rounded loveliness of her left breast.

My attention was caught by her supple grace and beauty. She was quite unlike the pockmarked, stoop-shouldered, sullen-faced girls and women who make up the bulk of El Berqa's population of prostitutes. I paused, and in that moment she let the rest of her robe fall open, giving me a quick glimpse of breasts, thighs, hips, an elegant and lovely body, and then the robe was closed again.

"Seven hundred fifty mils, American," she said.

I shook my head. Seven fifty mils was $1.50, which was a reasonable enough price for this Arab beauty. And for no more than a few pounds I could have her the full night.

But I wasn't interested. No matter how beautiful she was, I didn't want her badly enough to risk disease. But she *could* be of some use to me.

She took my hand and slipped it into her robe, pressing her warm

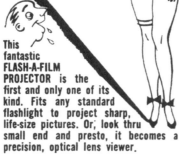

breast against it. I withdrew the hand. I was here to look, not to touch or to do. I took a one-pound note from my pocket. Her eyes began to glitter.

"You speak English?" I asked.

"Yes."

"All right, then. I'll give you this bill if you'll talk to me for a while. Nothing else but talk."

She looked at me strangely. I suppose she thought I was perverted or impotent, but I wasn't worried about that. Neither was she, really. She was for sale, and if I chose not to make use of her body that was my business. After a moment of puzzled hesitation she grinned, took the bill from me, and said, "All right. Come upstairs."

She led me up to her room on the second floor. It wasn't pretty. The walls were of cement, uncovered by plaster, and a single bare light bulb illuminated the room. There was a bed and a washbasin. She sat down on the bed. I remained standing. She gestured as if to remove her clothing, and her breasts were bare before I said, "No, I really just want to talk. I'm writing a magazine article on El Berqa."

"An American magazine?"

"Yes."

She was impressed. Instantly she was aglow, ready to tell me anything. Her name, she said, was Nadjia. She did not know her age, but thought she was about fifteen.

"How long have you been a prostitute?"

She shrugged. "Six—seven—eight years."

"You mean you began when you were *seven*?" I gasped, incredulous.

She smiled sadly. "In Cairo there are many men who will sleep only with young girls. A child of seven who is a skilled lover will earn many pounds, be in great demand. My price has gone down as I grew older."

"How did you—begin?"

"I was born in El Berqa. My mother was a prostitute too, and when I was old enough she began selling me. I have never known any other life. I have never been outside Cairo."

That explained, I thought, how such a beautiful girl could drift into prostitution. She had simply never known any other life. Just as simple as that. Going into prostitution at the age of seven was as natural for her as it was for an American boy to enter his Dad's firm when he grew up.

"Do you enjoy making love?" I asked.

Her answer was a mocking snort of laughter. "Do you *enjoy* breathing? I make love because I must, in order to earn my food. It is not a question of enjoying."

"But you pretend to enjoy it, when you're with a man?"

"If I like him, I make him feel that he is giving me pleasure. But I feel nothing, really."

"How much do you earn?"

"Sometimes a few mils, sometimes five pounds a night. The competition is very heavy here. But I am one of the lucky ones, for I am young and attractive. The older ones sometimes go hungry for days."

There were dozens of other things I wanted to ask her, about pimping in El Berqa, about her hopes for the future, about possible interference from the Nasser government. But she stood up abruptly, interrupting what had been a very pleasant, relaxed conversation, and said, in a suddenly businesslike voice, "You have had one pound's worth of time. Now you must go."

She ushered me to the door. I was tempted to offer her more money for a few more minutes of talk, but decided against it. I was growing ill at ease in this terribly drab room, and I had decided anyway that I had seen about enough of El Berqa.

At the door she said, "You will write about me in an American magazine?"

"Yes, Farida."

"I will be famous in America, far across the sea."

I nodded, and offered to send her a copy of the article when it was published. But she shook her head. She was unable to read, for one thing, and for another the other women would mock and curse her in jealousy if they found out. So she did not want a copy. As I started down the stairs I turned and said, "One more question?"

"What is it?"

"I want to know about whether the new government of President Nasser has interfered in any way with life in El Berqa."

Her beautiful eyes focussed clearly on me for a moment. Then she smiled and said, "*What* new government?" She laughed. "Everything is the same here as it always has been. It will always be the same."

With those words in my ears, I made my way to the street and headed out of El Berqa, hindered every step of the way by the loathsome peddlers and hawkers, and by the slimy pimps and sore-infested little boys trying to make a sale of womanflesh. Shooing them all away, I passed through the gates of El Berqa and out into Cairo proper.

I hope I've made it clear that it's foolish to believe the things that the Nasser propaganda machine churns out. Maybe there are a couple of new buildings in Cairo, and maybe the regime isn't quite as infested with corruption as was the Farouk bunch. But nothing essential has changed in Cairo—and certainly not El Berqa, the walled city in the heart of Cairo, the city of drug-peddling and pornographic peddling and pimping, the city of conspirators and disease-carriers and the city of beautiful fifteen-year-old prostitutes who have been selling their bodies since the age of seven. The name of the country has changed, but that's all. Nadjia's words are a sharp indictment of President Nasser. "*What* new government? Everything is the same here as it always has been. It will always be the same."

I think Nadjia is right. El Berqa, city of sin, was doing a bustling trade when America was populated only by Indians, and I think it will go on in the same way, new government or old, so long as there is an Egypt and so long as there are men willing to pay for the peculiar pleasures El Berqa offers.

The end

By *Sam Mallory*

RADIANT JADE:

THE CHINESE MATA HARI

She was known as the World's Most Vicious Woman, until that day in 1948 when an executioner's bullet ended her treacherous life. Spy, informer, harlot, seductress, torturer—the Manchu princess known as Radiant Jade was all of these. In her forty-one years she embraced every form of evil known to the Orient—and that takes in quite a range.

Daughter of Prince Su of China by one of his sixty concubines, Radiant Jade—Chin Pi-hui in Chinese—spent the first years of her life in the immense sprawling palace of her father in Peking, where even as an infant she was able to witness fantastic scenes of corruption at the decadent Chinese court. But that life soon was to change; in 1911 bloody revolution swept China, toppling the corrupt princess of the Manchu Dynasty from the Dragon Throne. The palace of Prince Su was sacked by kill-hungry rebels. Radiant Jade, then four, was hidden by a nurse. All other occupants of the palace were massacred, Jade alone surviving. History had chosen her to play a role of infamy.

In the years of confusion that followed the establishment of the new Chinese Republic, Radiant Jade escaped slaughter through the good offices of family servants who smuggled her to the city of Port Arthur, in

(Continued on page 68)

She was more beautiful,

more cunning, than her

World War I European

counterpart—the original

Mata Hari. But she was

much more deadly and cruel

beyond belief.

To insure the extraction of information from her prisoners; she used her most infamous torture: The Death of a Thousand Delights.

67

Manchuria—a cosmopolitan city with a large Russian and Japanese population. There she was adopted by a Japanese named Kawashima, who changed her name to Yoshiko—"Beautiful one."

Kawashima raised the young girl on the Spartan code of Japan's *samurai*, the warrior caste. Much of her later, nefarious success was due to the combination of her melting beauty and her rigid military discipline. But her Japanese foster-father saw other uses for the ex-Princess. As Radiant Jade ripened into a woman, maturing early as many Orientals do, Kawashima yearned for her budding breasts and expanding hips, and she had not yet reached her teens before she became a sharer of her foster-father's bed. Kawashima, as her first lover, instructed young Radiant Jade in the arts of love with a master's skill.

He was making an investment in the body of his sub-teen mistress—an investment that soon paid off handsomely. It was now the years between the World Wars, the years in which the Sons of the Rising Sun were laying the groundwork for their plot to conquer all of Asia. Kawashima was a high-ranking secret agent, working on the blueprint for conquest. And Radiant Jade, capable of speaking Russian, Japanese, and Korean fluently, as well as her own North China dialect, was invaluable to him.

Her first major assignment was marriage to the Prince of Tsitsihar. Japan, intending to gain control of Inner Mongolia, had selected the Prince to serve as a Nipponese puppet. The plan was for the Prince, a descendant of Mongol leader Genghis Khan, to lead his hordes in the conquest of Siberia and Mongolia, putting that vast land mass in Jap possession. And Radiant Jade, coached by the shrewd Nips, was supposed to be the Prince's inspiration, the power back of the throne.

The plan, however, fizzled. The Mongol prince was a bathless nomad whose court was held in a tent and whose ideas of sex involved brutal treatment of the delicate Chinese girl. Fed up with being manhandled, Radiant Jade left her unwashed spouse and headed for Old Peking. By this time she had matured into a breathtaking Oriental siren, slim and lissome of body, with breasts that fitted neatly into a cupping hand, and smooth, silken yellow skin.

She found Peking much to her liking. When the Prince of Tsitsihar came in search of her after several years, he found her dwelling in a magnificent palace, waited on by a handpicked staff of a dozen young boys who took turns as bed-fellows for the voluptuous, youthful spy.

And she was in the thick of every spy maneuver taking place in Peking in the late '20s and early '30s. Her fancy love-nest doubled as GHQ for Japan's devilish secret agents, as well as rebellious Chinese warlords and White Russian exiles plotting to uproot Communist rule in Siberia. Radiant Jane played hostess to all of them, deftly extricating their secrets and peddling them around. Few men could remain tight-lipped in Radiant Jade's presence. A few artful caresses and she drew a man's innermost secrets. And if neither *amour* nor liquor nor opium could loosen a man's tongue, Radiant Jade had even more effective methods of obtaining information. Heiress to four thousand years of Asiatic cruelty, she was a past mistress in the unholy art of torture.

Deep within her high-walled palace were the torture chambers of Radiant Jade. Schooled by experts, she practiced her craft on any hapless victims that came her way.

One of her favorites was the Death of a Thousand Delights—inconceivable to Western minds, a torture that involved such extremes of pleasure and pain that the victim's mind eventually gave way. Less subtle but equally effective was the Room of the Rats, in which a man would be spreadeagled, naked, while a pack of voracious rats was loosed to devour his living flesh. Jade would stand by, frequently nude herself, her lovely body glistening brightly with oils, and her silver laughter would tinkle in the torture cell as the vicious rats devoured a prisoner's delicate parts.

The most sadistic of all Radiant Jade's repertoire was one she used only four times—in 1930, 1931, and twice the following year: "The Gloves."

It was the second performance of this torment that helped build Radiant Jade's reputation. She staged it before a carefully chosen audience of comrade spies and schemers. A Manchurian warlord and his general staff were paying a visit to Peking, and Radiant Jade had been commissioned to pry from him the strategy of a coming struggle between the warlords of Manchuria. Knowing that only the ultimate in torture would yield the secrets, Radiant Jade made careful preparations.

The guests were plied with women, wine, and opium, to no effect. Their secrets remained locked in their skulls. Telling them, then, that she would conduct them on a personal tour through her museum of erotica, Jade escorted her victims to a luxurious anteroom occupied by nude dancing girls and an accompanying orchestra. While the dancers writhed, Jade's audience gathered to watch the fun. And behind carved doors, huge kettles of water were coming to a boil.

At a signal, a massive bronze gong sounded resonantly; the doors were flung open, and the warlord and his staff, lulled by drugs and drink, were seized by Radiant Jade's servants and were thrust forward to be held over the boiling kettles.

"Will you tell us what we want

PORTABLE TRANSISTOR RADIO FOR ONLY $7.95

No Tubes To Replace! Nothing To Plug In.
Plays Beautifully On One 10c Battery!

GUARANTEED TO OUT-PERFORM ANY RADIO IT'S PRICE-AND-SIZE IN THE WORLD TODAY
OR MONEY BACK!

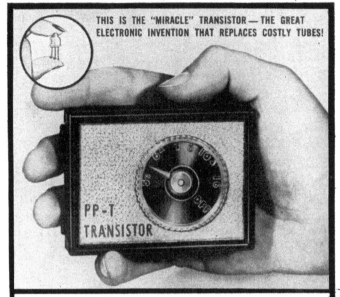

THIS IS THE "MIRACLE" TRANSISTOR — THE GREAT ELECTRONIC INVENTION THAT REPLACES COSTLY TUBES!

PP-T TRANSISTOR

The most fabulous radio value ever offered! A precision-engineered, American-made transistor portable with amazingly beautiful tone! So tiny in size, it fits in the palm of your hand . . so big in entertainment value you'll never want to be without it wherever you are, whatever you're doing!

It's small, it's good-looking, it plays like a dream! Gives you incredibly loud, clear reception.

Called the PP-T Transistor Portable, this amazing set actually plays for a thousand hours on just one 10c battery! That's almost 3 hours of non-stop playing per day, every day for a full year — a cost of about a penny a month!

The PP-T is new, it's different, it's practical and the cost is so amazingly low, you will hardly believe it in this day and age — truly a once-in-a-lifetime opportunity to own a transistor portable at such an incredibly low price!

Just imagine the thrill! You turn the dial and immediately — no warm up, no waiting — you hear music, news, sports programs as loud and as clear as a bell!

It's really amazing! At home, at work, at play, a personal, transistor portable right at your finger-tips!

It's so tiny you can tuck it in your shirt pocket just like a pack of cigarettes . . . carry it in your handbag just like a compact! Enjoy it at home, take it to the ballgame and other sporting events, bring it along on vacations, picnics, to the beach, on dates, wherever you like! Your family will love it, your friends will be amazed, the kids will gasp in astonishment at the fabulous performance and handsome good-looks of your wonderful PP-T — and of course they'll ask

HOW CAN A TRANSISTOR RADIO COST SO LITTLE?

The PP-T Portable Radio is new, different, precision-made in vast quantities by one of the pioneers in the transistor field. There is no high import duty to pay because it's American made! Ingenious, time-saving production techniques and an amazingly simplified electronic circuit make it possible to bring you the PP-T Radio at such incredible savings! Fewer parts, less labor costs through more efficient assembly, and you save the big difference!

BRILLIANT ENGINEERING MAKES THE BIG DIFFERENCE!

Your PP-T is a marvel of engineering ingenuity. For example, you know that the heart of our aircraft, guided missile and communications systems is electronics. Scientists, in their never-ending search for newer, lighter and more powerful radio components, have employed two fabulous devices.

Both are featured in the PP-T.

One is, of course, the miracle transistor you've heard so much about! It's a tiny, electronic device smaller than your fingernail, and yet so amazingly effective, it takes the place of bulky, complicated radio tubes and outlasts them many, many times over!

Then there is the germanium diode . . . an electronic component being used by the Army and Navy in Radar and Sonar. This ultra-sensitive device has the incredible ability to pick radio waves right from the air!

Instead of the cumbersome, parts-packed radios you are accustomed to, now you have a magnificent transistor portable smaller than a pack of cigarettes, lighter than a deck of cards, less expensive by far than even the cheapest imported transistor sets you can buy! That's the secret

EXCLUSIVE ELECTRONIC CIRCUIT FOR BETTER LISTENING!

Your PP-T is a tiny personal portable incorporating the very latest design features! It comes with a tiny electronic ear speaker and that's one of the big advantages! You put the ear speaker in your ear and your set is truly personal!

At home, let the rest of the family make as much noise as they want to! You hear your popular programs clearly, perfectly! At sport events, let the crowds roar! You hear perfectly. At night, listen to your personal portable as late as you like. You won't disturb a soul! Whatever you're doing — even on the job — you can enjoy sporting events, good music, and dramatic shows without disturbing anyone else.

That's a positive fact! You aren't buying promises . . You are buying results! The PP-T is beautifully designed . . It's beautifully made! It plays like a dream! It's an instrument you'll use and enjoy for years and years to come!

And now this wonderful set is available to you — a rugged, all-purpose portable . . handy, compact, good-looking! A wonderful set, a wonderful value, at a price you just can't afford to miss out on!

THE REST IS UP TO YOU!

We've told you how the set works. We've shown you how it looks. We've detailed the reasons why we can bring it to you at such an incredible saving. We know that if we could attach it to this magazine page so you could see it, feel it, hear it play, you'd buy it in a minute! But because that isn't possible, the only way you can know the thrill of hearing it and seeing it, is by actually sending for it. And since we are so anxious for you to do just that, we make this special

10 DAY NO-RISK TRIAL OFFER

Send for your PP-T transistor radio now! If it isn't more wonderful than we say — if you aren't amazed at the value — if you aren't delighted at the low cost — if you and your entire family aren't thrilled at the fantastic performance, don't keep it!

Simply return this radio to us for a complete refund! For the few pennies your home trial has cost, you've had the satisfaction of seeing it, using it and showing it to your family and friends.

We make this offer because we know once you hear this radio, once you use it you'll never want to be without it!

Why not take advantage of this wonderful opportunity right now? Why not give yourself the satisfaction of at least finding out?

So don't put it off. If you'd like to try this wonderful little radio, make up your mind now! Don't hesitate or delay because supplies are limited. Simply fill out the coupon right now and mail it at once. Or better still, stop in today!

DON'T BE CONFUSED! This is the first time the PP-T Personal Portable Transistor Radio has ever been advertised! Don't confuse this precision-made transistor set with weak Crystal sets. PP-T is the product of a large, experienced radio manufacturer — a specialist in transistor sets whose superb engineering skills, technical, know-how and vast production facilities have combined to bring you what is unquestionably the finest radio value in the world today.

NEVER A TRANSISTOR VALUE LIKE THIS:

Tiny in Size — Tremendous in Performance
Compare These Outstanding Features!
ONLY $7.95

- **Precision Engineered** — for amazingly fine tone and volume — "the most for the money" in a transistor radio.
- **Transistor Amplifier** — designed to outlast tubes many times over.
- **Tiny, Button-Type Ear Speaker** — for completely private listening.
- **Handsome Polystyrene Case** — with rich gold-toned radio Grill hardly bigger than a cigarette case. Beautiful and expensive looking. Small enough to slip in shirt pocket.
- **Selective Tuning System** — with special Hi-Q Ferrite Slug Tuner for remarkable selectivity.
- **"Clip-Tenna"** — Handy antenna can be clipped to many common metal objects—pipes, posts, telephone dial, radiator, screens, auto-trim, etc., depending on where you happen to be!
- **10c Battery** — Plays up to 1000 hours non-stop. Drain so small you don't even have to turn set off if you don't want to. Case snaps open for easy access to battery.

Remember — PP-T is not a weak, old-fashioned crystal set, but a beautifully engineered and manufactured, transistorized radio, guaranteed to outperform any radio its price and size in the world — or your money back!

Cardiff-Hall Electronics, Dept DEPT. EX-1   480 Lexington Ave. New York 17, N. Y.

Cardiff-Hall Electronics,   Dept. EX-1
480 Lexington Ave   New York 17, N. Y.

Rush my PP-T Personal Portable Transistor Radio at once! If I don't agree this is the most wonderful radio value ever, I will return my set for a complete refund, no questions asked.

☐ I enclose $7.95 on money-back guarantee (You pay all postage charges)

☐ I enclose $14.90 for two PP-T radios. (One for me, one for a friend). I save $1 and you pay all postage charges.

(Please Print Carefully)

Name _____

Address _____

City _____ State _____

☐ Please send C.O.D. I will pay postman $7.95 plus C.O.D. postage and handling. Same money-back guarantee, of course!

69

know?" Jade asked casually.

A furious command from the warlord silenced the staff. Jade shrugged; she knew she would get her information anyway, and now she would have her sadistic pleasure as well. At a signal, the tunics were ripped from her captives. The warlord, two of his generals, three colonels, and a captain, all remaining silent, were led forward to the kettles. One by one, beginning with the warlord, the arms of the men were thrust into the sizzling water. The men screamed in agony, but the limbs were held in place. Within minutes, the flesh of their arms was scalded. Seeing what was in store for them, the captain and one of the colonels cracked; they babbled that they would talk, and they were led away for questioning. For the rest, the torture continued. While Jade and her guests rollicked with laughter, the cooked arms were taken from the kettle and Jade's eunuch servants carefully peeled the skin off, beginning at the shoulder. They removed it expertly, revealing the partly boiled flesh beneath. Even the skin of the tips of the fingers was peeled away, glove-fashion.

Then, half-naked, the officers were thrust into the courtyard. It was the middle of winter; the thermometer was close to zero. Like fish in a deep freeze the flayed arms, bare and bloody, froze almost at once. While Jade's orchestra struck up a merry tune, the Manchurians rolled in the snow, screaming in awful agony, until consciousness left them. As they lay, freezing to death in the winter night, Radiant Jade and her guests returned to the warmth within to continue their feastmaking and jolly festivities.

On her next performance of "The Gloves," Jade introduced a variation by staging it in the summer. Instead of being frozen, the victims' torture was heightened by the swarms of flies that lighted on their raw flesh, to Radiant Jade's great delight!

Her stay in Peking ended virtually overnight. Quietly, in the dark, Jade and her entourage stole away, for reasons no one will ever know, leaving her palace dark and padlocked. She turned up next in Port Arthur, disguised as a man, serving as aide-de-camp to a Japanese general. Jade and her general went on a spying tour in Manchuria, posing as commercial agents looking for business opportunities. But the Japanese general complained of little success; he could not penetrate deeply into the secrets of the Chinese military defenses.

Here Radiant Jade was valuable. Since she was a nymphomaniac with an insatiable lust for men, it scarcely displeased her to pose temporarily as a prostitute. With much publicity she was installed in a Mukden bordello much frequented by high-ranking Chinese officers. She posed as a Korean, this time.

Within a short time her erotic talents had made her the star attraction of the house. The Chinese colonels vied with each other for the right to sleep with the sinuous seductress. They heaped her with gifts, and then, in the bedroom, Jade would first dazzle them with all the sexual arts at her command, and then persuade them craftily to spill valuable secrets. When she left Mukden, not long after, she took with her two dozen chests of gold and pearls and jade—and, also, the hidden secrets of the Chinese high command.

Not much afterward the Japanese, greatly aided by the secrets Radiant Jade had stolen for them, pounced on sleepy China, occupying the entire North. Radiant Jade returned in triumph to Peking, reopening her palace and once again playing hostess to Oriental orgies on a monumental scale. A new wrinkle was added, now: Radiant Jade promoted herself to the rank of General. Calling herself *Sze-ling*—"General"—she dressed in gaudy military costume, replete with medals, sword, and high boots. Rumor has it that she went through a lesbian phase at this time, summoning Pekinese beauties who thought they

would be sleeping with a male general, and then forcing them to submit to her unnatural desires. In the evenings, however, Jade reverted to her silken robes and her feminine wiles.

In the late 1930s, as Japan marched southward through China, Radiant Jade accepted a new spying assignment. She became a "male" Chinese soldier behind the front defenses of Shanghai. Spying by day, changing clothes and becoming the mistress of the Chinese leaders at night, she relayed information to the Japanese conquerors that laid Shanghai open for capture.

The whereabouts of Radiant Jade during the Second World War are uncertain. We know that at times she served in the forces on Chiang Kai-Shek, spying on him for the benefit of her Japanese masters. Later in the war, as the tide began to turn against Nippon, she sold Japanese military secrets to the Soviet Union. But she betrayed Russia, too, by carrying out spy duties for the White Russian enemies of Stalin's regime.

Late in the Second World War it became apparent to Radiant Jade's various employers that she was deceiving them all, peddling anyone's secrets to anyone. Abruptly, Jade fell from favor. She had always lived lavishly, and now she had nothing left.

She returned to Peking. It was near the end of the war, now. Japan's defeat was inevitable. Radiant Jade was thirty-seven, and tired. Twenty-five years of debauchery and sin had left their mark on her body, once so sleek and seductive. She was still a beautiful woman, but, almost between one day and the next, she began to age rapidly.

Establishing herself in a dingy little house in a slum section of Peking, Radiant Jade hired herself out as a prostitute—not for gold and pearls now, but for a few miserable copper coins. The body that had delighted warlords and generals now writhed obediently for the satisfaction of the lusts of foul-smelling peasants. What money she earned was spent for opium. She did not dare attract attention to herself, for fear of discovery.

But, one day after the end of the war, a high-ranking member of Chiang Kai-Shek's staff was passing through the quarter of Peking where Jade lived. He thought he recognized her, as she stood beckoning to prospective clients from her doorway. But he was not sure. Following her in, he paid the pitiful sum she asked; she dropped her robe, standing before him nude, and drew him down to the miserable bed.

After making love to her, the officer had no doubt. This haggard woman of forty was Radiant Jade. Her body had lost its beauty, but not its skill. Weeping, Jade admitted her identity and was taken into custody.

"You, more than any other single person, are responsible for China's tragedy," her judge thundered at her. Jade was thrown into a drab, filthy prison. There, she was given the infamous Chinese "soft" and "hard" treatment.

During the "soft" periods, she was given all the liquor she could hold, all the opium she craved, all the morphine she desired. A white man, one of Chiang Kai-Shek's disreputable American adventurers, entered her cell and made love to her, prolonging the act for hours, seemingly. While under the influence of drugs or liquor, anything Jade babbled was jotted down to be used as evidence.

Then, without notice, the "hard" period would begin. The dozen pipes of opium, the daily shots of morphine were denied her. Hellish withdrawal pains racked her body as day after day she writhed in torment. Her white lover entered her cell and stimulated her to the brink of ecstasy, without permitting her satisfaction. Or he would strip off his belt and mercilessly beat her nude body.

For months the alternation of "hard" and "soft" treatment continued, while Radiant Jade lived in agony no less severe than any suffered by the victims of the rats or "The Gloves." She pleaded for death. Instead, all she got was the dreaded alternation of pleasure and pain, never knowing when one period would end and the

other begin. Torment and torture seemed to go on eternally.

At last, in March, 1948, Radiant Jade's tormentors decided she had suffered long enough for her vicious crimes against China. She was brought to trial, a haggard, shuffling wreck of the one-time queen of lust. The trial was swift. The Hopei High Court sentenced her to die a traitor's death.

Two weeks later, she was roughly dragged into the prison courtyard at dawn. Hands bound behind her back she was thrust down on her knees in the mud. A cold gunmuzzle was placed behind her left ear. A single shot was fired.

Toppling forward, face first, she lay dead, the breasts caressed by monarchs now pressed against cold mud. Her body was stripped of its rags; the jailers, curious to see the corpse of this royal princess who had been the boldest of spies and courtesans, crowded around. Then she was tossed into a grave in a corner of the prison yard. She had lived excitingly, and had died a dog's death. Like her European counterpart of World War I, Mata Hari, Radiant Jade paid for her treachery with her life. But even now, more than a decade after her execution, she is still remembered with awe and fear by the peoples of Asia.

The end

Special: VISIT AN OPIUM DEN IN VIET NAM!

EXOTIC

Adventures

aSn

VOL. 1
NO. 5

50¢

THE ARABIAN SLAVE-GIRL RACKET

ISLAND OF LOVE-STARVED WOMEN

TERROR IN THE FAR EAST:
THE WOLF-WOMEN OF INDIA

Plus:
MISS
BERLIN:
FABULOUS,
FANTASTIC,
EXOTIC!

by

Len Patterson

74

gallant, postponing things till the wedding night. Her arm tightened possessively round my waist as we entered the dance hall, and she proceeded to tell all her chums of our engagement.

I drew her away into the corner. "You've been making a mistake, Daphne. I can't marry you!"

"You mean you lied when you said you were married?"

"No, but—I don't *want* to get married! I thought we would just have a good time, up on that cliff. It's all a big misunderstanding!"

She was shocked and tearful, and insisted I would have to explain everything to her parents. It seems that she had proudly announced, earlier in the day, that she had hooked herself a man.

I walked with her to her parents' house. Her father greeted me sternly. He was very English-looking, and very grim-faced. He got even grimmer as I explained that I hadn't realized that by putting my arm around Daphne in the jeep I was proposing marriage. "In my country," I jabbered, "we aren't so black-and-white about these things. A little necking and petting doesn't mean a proposal."

"Have you known my daughter?" he thundered.

"No, sir," I said, thanking my lucky stars that Daphne had told me the real situation before I had done anything permanent. And she backed me up.

The fact that I hadn't despoiled his daughter was some relief to the old man, but he still gave me a good chewing out. "If you travel, you must obey the customs of the land you visit," he roared. "A display of affection to an unmarried girl is a serious thing here." And so on for about half an hour, after which time he let me go with a warning to keep away from Daphne unless my intentions became strictly honorable.

I crept back to the dance hall with my ears burning. Ron had already departed with his Wilhelmina. But as I stood looking around for him, a bouncy little islander practically threw herself into my arms.

Her name was Anna, and she was married, and her husband was not due back from Curaçao for another three months. I made sure of those facts before I took another step. Then we danced for a while, and I was invited to her spotless little cottage for a drink of local wine, and while we were sipping it she casually unbuttoned her blouse and put my hands on her heavy, delicious breasts.

We made a grand old night of it; and in the morning she didn't want to let me go, but I managed to escape.

Ron and I remained on Saba for a full week, and only the fact that we had reservations on other islands made us reluctantly take our leave. And during that week, we had our hands full keeping the "Dutch widows" happy. We operated with a different one every night, and sometimes took afternoons as well. There were more than a hundred buxom lassies competing for our attention, and we did the best we could.

One thing I learned about Saba. There are two different types of man-hungry women there. One type is the Daphne sort—the girls who have not yet snared a husband. They're pretty desperate for some loving, but if you seduce them, you're expected to marry them. The other type is the Anna–Wilhelmina type: the married women whose ardor is undampened in the absence of their mates. Anything goes with these girls, and no obligation afterward.

So the trick is to find out in advance whether you're merely brightening the life of a lonely *frau* or signing yourself over to a lonelier *fraulein*. I had a narrow escape with Daphne. But I'm saving my pennies for a return trip. Maybe this time Daphne will have trapped that wandering Trinidad boy of hers, and he'll have come and gone, leaving Daphne pining for consolation. I think you can figure out the rest of what I have in mind.

The end

one of the married women, who could grant the same pleasures without any loss of honor. I was still gaping like a hooked fish when she let me know that she had saved her virginity for just this very moment, and I could have her on the spot—we wouldn't even have to wait for the wedding ceremony, which would take place the following Sunday.

There had been a mammoth misunderstanding. I told her that I didn't want to get intimate tonight, that I wanted to go back to the dance. I knew that once I did anything irreversible to this girl, I wouldn't get off the island with my skin intact.

So we went back to the dance. Daphne evidently figured I was being

OPIUM DEN IN VIETNAM

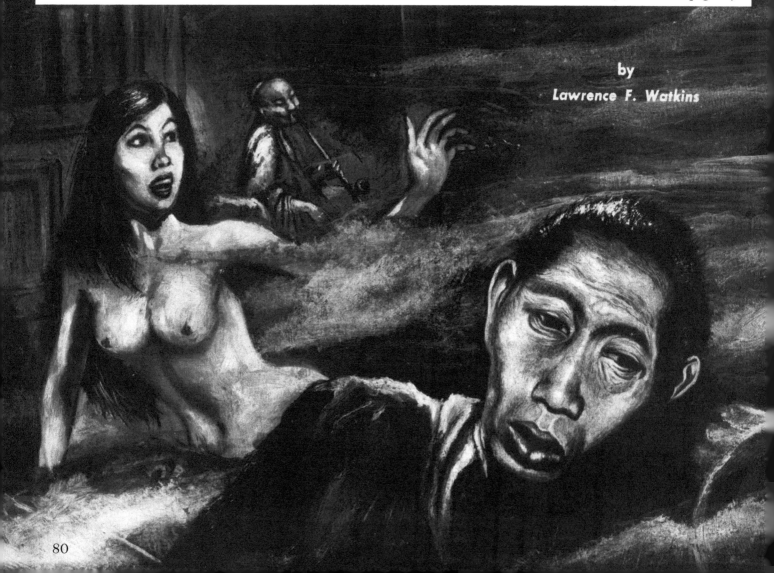

WHEN I told the editor of *Exotic Adventures* that I would shortly be leaving on a business trip to Saigon, the capital of the Republic of Vietnam, he immediately said, "Good. I want you to visit an opium den and give us a complete report."

His request shocked me. I had been to Saigon three times in the past four years, as a travelling representative of the rubber company for which I work. Each time, I had scrupulously avoided Saigon's numerous *fumeries*, or opium-smoking parlors, despite frequent invitations from Saigonese friends and business acquaintances to "come have a smoke." My curiosity was high, but I had the Westerner's fear of the sinister habit.

Nevertheless, I agreed to consider the idea. And before I left for Vietnam, I did some checking on opium addiction. I found that opium addiction is

(Continued on page 82)

by
Lawrence F. Watkins

The French Deputy Inspector led his American visitor into the interior of the dark and murky opium den. There, in the smoky gloom of the unreal world, he saw the half-naked girl reclining on the small wooden bench.

J.F. APGAR JR.

81

much more difficult to attain than addiction to other drugs. It takes six months, at least, of regular opium use before the weed becomes habitual. The harmful side effects of the habit take even longer to develop.

I was going to be in Saigon for only a few weeks—hardly long enough to develop the habit, and besides I intended to exercise complete self-control in my experiments with opium. Since the drug is not easily obtained in this country, I was running small risk of becoming an addict, provided I restrained myself and got out of Saigon at the right time.

And so I found myself bound for what had once been French Indochina, fully prepared to risk opium addiction for the sake of gratifying my curiosity and giving the readers of *Exotic Adventures* some information.

Making contact with the world of opium dens was the simplest thing imaginable. On my second night in Saigon, I dined with a French official who cheerfully suggested a visit to a *fumerie*.

"You really must smoke the pipe before you leave Saigon, *mon ami*. It is a fascinating experience—if you practice moderation!"

"All right," I said. I realized I was trembling. "Take me to a place you trust."

After dinner, he conducted me to a small dwelling in a winding back street. We ascended a staircase, and I could smell the opium as we climbed. I felt as nervous as a teenage boy about to make love for the first time.

There was no nonsense about passwords, secret peep-holes, or any other fol-de-rol. My French friend opened the door, signaled for me to enter, and followed me in.

The madame of the establishment came bustling to greet us—a plump,

smiling Chinese woman in her thirties, whose silken wrap was pulled tight over her breasts. Her skirt was slashed, as is the style, practically to the hip.

I listened as my friend told her in French, "It is his first time. He must have no more than he can stand."

"Certainly. I will let him have only four pipes. And you?"

"I will not smoke tonight," my friend said.

I began to lose some of my tension as I realized I was in friendly, sympathetic hands. I was guided to a hard couch, with a leather pillow hard as rock. I settled down, while the Chinese pipemaker prepared my first dose.

He stood by a small lamp, kneading a tiny ball of gum-like dope, toasting it over the flame at the end of a needle until it began to bubble. At the moment of bubbling, he thrust the little ball of opium into the pipe with the needle, and put the pipe in my hands.

As I had been instructed, I held the bowl of the pipe over the flame, and sucked in the smoke, deep into my lungs. Within less than half a minute, the pipe was out. I learned later that veteran opium smokers generally draw an entire pipeful into their lungs in one long gasp.

I noticed no immediate effect. But after the second pipe I felt a slight drowsiness; after the third, the world began to feel somewhat unreal; after the fourth, I felt alert but calm, wonderfully calm, with no fears for the future. I talked on and on, probably incoherently, to my French companion and to the madame. I remember being disappointed that they would not let me have another pipe.

"You will have the nausea if you take another, *cher ami!* Come, let us leave, tomorrow is another time."

We paid—it was ten piasters a pipe, which meant that with tips and all the visit had cost me hardly more than a dollar—and my friend drove me back to my hotel. "I will see you again tomorrow," he said. "If you are still interested in opium, there are other places to visit."

That night I experienced for the first time the strange repose of opium. I lay awake, utterly relaxed, with the taste of the smoke still on my tongue. I was so calm that I felt cut off from my body. *This is what it must be like to be a ghost*, I thought. And then, suddenly, I tumbled into the deepest sleep I had ever had. You do not dream after smoking opium, not until the next morning when the effects are leaving. Toward dawn, I had strange dreams of fanciful colors and weird shapes, and then I awoke, feeling completely refreshed. My first experience with opium had ended successfully.

After attending to my business affairs during that day, I again met my French friend for dinner. "Tonight," he said, "I will take you to two more *fumeries*. A very cheap one, and a more elegant one. Tomorrow I cannot see you, but later in the week I will take you to yet another—a very special one. You will enjoy it."

We clambered into his Peugeot sedan and drove off. Our first stop of the evening was in a shabby quarter of the city, at a *fumerie* in a dilapidated old wooden frame building. On the first floor, a dealer in goods from Communist China held forth. Above him was the opium den. It was a dingy place. The proprietor himself, an elderly Chinese, was an addict—"He smokes sixty pipes a day," my friend murmured. The man had the skeletal, dehydrated look of the longtime addict. Like most drugs, opium robs one of appetite, but provides no nourishment itself. The result is a skin-and-bones appearance.

As my eyes became accustomed to the dim light, I saw that the place had only a few other inhabitants. A middle-aged man was lost in dreamland; he, too, looked like an addict. A young girl, no more than nineteen, lay sprawled asleep on a couch, and a boy of her age, perhaps her lover, was sprawled asleep on the next one. In Saigon opium smokers remove much of their clothing when in a *fumerie*. The girl wore only a band of cloth round her hips. Her lovely young golden-brown breasts rose and fell slowly, but no one in the place paid any attention to her near nudity. Opium diminishes the sex impulse after a while, too.

We had two pipes apiece. The opium was rough, harsher than the stuff I had had the night before. No one said anything to us as we paid—twenty-five piasters apiece—and left.

"Why did you take me there?" I asked.

"You must get the complete view. The place we have just left is the most typical kind. There are many such small rooms, all over the city, with their regular clients and occasional youngsters. No one speaks, no one looks up; the business of smoking opium is all that matters there."

We motored across town next to a substantially more attractive section of town, and pulled up in front of an imposing building with a colorful Oriental front.

"This is one of the more exclusive *fumeries*," my friend informed me. "Thirty piastres a pipe, and you must make reservations in advance. Here you may have a private booth if you wish to entertain a lady friend intimately, but the management does not supply girls themselves."

We entered. The familiar smell of opium hung over the place. But the furnishings were beautiful, and paintings in elaborate frames hung on the walls; an enormous bookshelf held volumes in eight or ten languages. The place looked like nothing so much as a high-class bordello, except that the commodity being peddled here was not female flesh but drug-induced dreaming.

"The opium here is of the best," my friend said as we settled down on our couches, and he was right. Even with my limited knowledge of the subject, I could tell that this opium was as superior to the stuff we had had previously as a fine bottle of vintage Burgundy is to a jug of cheap red wine. The pipes bubbled softly over the flame, and the gentle perfume of the drug filled my nostrils. I felt the familiar calm coming over me, and I could readily understand the attraction of this drug. In

a confused and strife-torn world, the opium smokers were gladly willing to tolerate the inevitable physical, moral, and mental deterioration that the weed brings, in return for the tranquility it yields.

Later we returned to my hotel, and once again that night I experienced the complete calm that I had known the night before.

My appetite was scanty the next day, and I felt lightheaded and gay. The experience opened my eyes to the real danger of the drug. I was relieved that my French companion would be busy tonight, for I didn't want to overdo my indoctrination. I was grateful, too, for the fact that I would be back in the States within a couple of weeks, far from the temptations of the *fumeries*.

In the course of my day's business I was more alert to the symptoms of addiction. One of the executives I met with that day had the thin bony look of the addict, and he admitted as much to me. "I have had the habit thirty years," he said. "Within five years more, it

will destroy me. But I cannot say I am sorry."

He offered to take me to *his* favorite *fumerie* that night, but I politely declined. He was a connoisseur of opium, who could discourse learnedly on the different kinds—Istanbul opium, Benares opium, Laos opium, Yunan opium. I knew it would be dangerous for me to get involved with him.

The next night, when my faithful French companion arrived at my hotel to pick me up, he had two companions with him—one of them a halfcaste Eurasian, the other a Vietnamese, and both of them wearing the badge of the local police!

For a dizzy moment I thought I was being arrested. But my friend explained quickly.

"These gentlemen are comrades of mine. They will join us on our little tour this night. We will be much safer in their company."

The four of us set out to explore the night life of Saigon. My friend had promised something special this

time, and he kept his word. We drove to the *paillote* district—a region of thatched tumbledown houses, very sinister-looking. I was glad that there were four of us. We entered a court-yard and discovered a complete social center—a restaurant, a cafe-bar, a brothel, and a *fumerie*.

We entered the *fumerie*. It was run by a young Chinese madame, dressed in a stiff high-collared dress. Her face had the serene radiance of a goddess. I was introduced to her in French as an American novice in the arts of the orient, and she said in perfect English, "You will be well entertained here. I will see to that."

We were led up a wooden ladder to rooms upstairs, partitioned off to afford privacy. I was shown into one of the little sections, and my companions entered areas across the way. A broad double mattress, covered with a fresh white sheet, lay on the floor, and on a little stand were the usual pipe-making paraphernalia.

For perhaps ten minutes I lay on the mattress, wondering if I were supposed to prepare my pipe myself, something which I did not know how to do. But then the door opened and a girl entered. She was a Vietnamese, perhaps twenty, with long glossy black hair. She wore a thin kimono through which I could make out the curves of her handsome body. Kneeling by the stand, she smiled at me and said in French, "I will prepare your pipes."

"I thought men did that job."

"A pipe prepared by a woman is more sweet," she said. She went through the manipulations and handed me a lit pipe. I inhaled it quickly; while I relaxed afterward, I realized that the girl was removing my shoes, which I had forgotten to do. I was too relaxed to stop her—even when she proceeded to remove my trousers as well.

Lying there in my underwear, I accepted a second pipe from her. The effects of opium are cumulative, and the second pipe is more powerful than the first. I half-shut my eyes.

To my surprise, I became aware that the girl had slipped out of her kimono. She was nude beneath it, and with an objective eye I studied the full-ness of her tawny breasts, the delicate coloring of her hips, thighs, buttocks. She was altogether beautiful. But I didn't expect it when she lay down next to me on the broad mattress and murmured, "Shall we make love now or after the next pipe?"

Opium-drugged as I was, I still managed to struggle up to a sitting position and look surprised.

"I didn't ask for a woman!"

"But—they told me you wanted one," she exclaimed piteously, her head dropping. "You don't want me?"

I did, to be honest, but I was uneasy about getting mixed up with Oriental prostitutes. I had been lucky all my life in avoiding the diseases of love, but this was no time to push my luck. No matter how attractive this girl was, no matter how delightful the promise of her rounded breasts and broad hips, I wasn't taking any chances.

She was heartbroken, or perhaps she was just afraid of getting scolded by her employer later, but finally she left, tears in her eyes.

A few minutes later my door opened again. This time it was ma-dame herself who entered and knelt by me.

"The girl did not please you?" she asked.

"You don't understand—"

"But your friends told me to get the best for you," she said. "I selected her myself."

I shook my head. "She's a lovely-looking girl. But the risk of disease, you know—"

She nodded understandingly. "May I make you a pipe?"

She prepared the pipe with her own hands. I smoked three more in rapid succession, making five altogeth-er, and I was beginning to get intoxi-cated with the drug. And my hostess latched the door and started to remove her clothes.

I was too far gone to protest. And I knew she was treating me to a rare honor, the favors of the proprietress herself. Since her finest girl had not pleased me, she could redeem the honor of her establishment only by entertaining me herself.

Beneath the stiff formality of her clothing, her body was young and lithe, the breasts small but perfectly formed, the legs flawless. I knew it would be a deadly insult for me to refuse her. She made love to me won-derfully, in an Oriental manner I had never experienced before. It was all done with the utmost delicacy; she did not even permit me to touch her breasts. When it was over, she dressed and made three more pipes for me, my sixth, seventh, and eighth of the evening.

I dozed off after that, and some time later my friends came to get me. In the car, downstairs, my companion asked me how the night had gone.

"It was glorious," I said dream-ily. I told them of how I had ner-vously repulsed the attentions of the prostitute, and how the madame her-self had come to attend to me.

They slapped me on the back, con-gratulating me heartily. It seemed that the beautiful young proprietor was no prostitute herself, and could not be had for any price. On rare occasions, she had been known to give herself volun-tarily. And it had been my great luck to experience one of those occasions.

I decided to quit while I was ahead. I was deliciously refreshed by the events of the evening, but the effects of the eight pipes made me worthless the next day. For the rest of my stay in Saigon, I kept scrupulously away from the *fumeries*.

And so my experience with opium was an educational and interesting one. But I feel no desire at all to renew my acquaintance with the drug. I remember all too well the sight of the shambling, fleshless lifetime addicts, doomed to live in a half-world of dreams.

The end

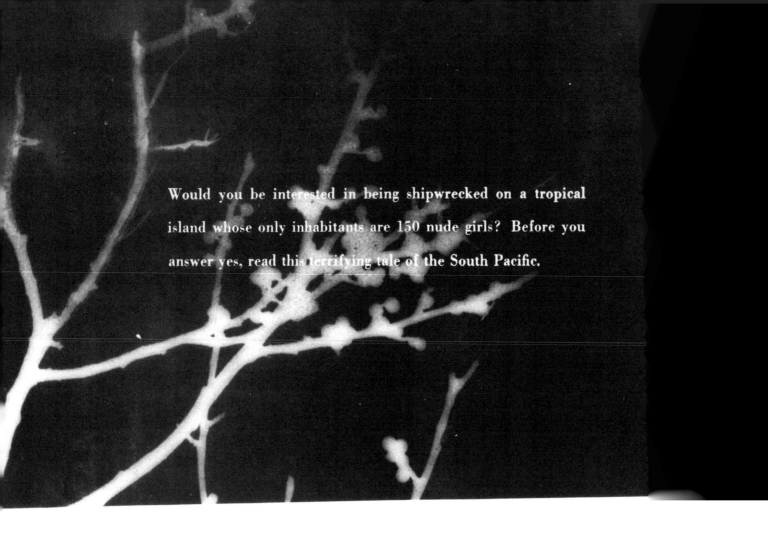

Would you be interested in being shipwrecked on a tropical island whose only inhabitants are 150 nude girls? Before you answer yes, read this terrifying tale of the South Pacific.

by *Lin Charles*
as told to Sam Mallory

ISLAND OF EXILED WOMEN

SHIPWRECKED on a tropic isle in the South Pacific, your only companions some two hundred fifty beautiful nude girls hungry for your caresses—that sounds like paradise on Earth, doesn't it? The sort of thing every red-blooded man dreams about.

Well, let me give you the *real* scoop, buddy, because I've been through it. It isn't paradise at all. It's hell, sheer mucking hell, after the first half hour. It isn't a dream, it's a nightmare. And if you don't think so, go try it for yourself.

The island is still there. The girls will be mostly different, because it's five years since the time of my visit,

but whoever is there now will be just as lovely and just as amorous.

The name of the island is Luanape. It's a bit of coral rock not quite a mile square, located in the Gilbert Islands.

The women range from about age sixteen to about age thirty. They are drawn from most of the islands in the area, and some from as far away as the Marshall islands to the north and the Ellice group to the south. You see, Luanape is a kind of prison island. The natives send women there who have to be exiled from their tribes for any one of a number of sexual offenses.

A woman who spends the night

(Continued on page 88)

with a lover, becomes pregnant, and refuses to name the man, is likely to draw a six-months sentence of exile on Luanape. Contrariwise, a girl who is visited by a "creeping rapist" at night (the *moetotolo*) and who tries to protect him or herself by keeping quiet, she can get three months. The girl who *does* name her lover against his wishes is packed off for seven months, and if she names an innocent party, she can get a year.

An island belle who is unfaithful to her husband behind his back gets sentenced; so does one who declines to sleep with any man her husband may choose to lend her to. A girl who takes excessive pleasure in the act of love may get sent to Luanape to have her ardor cooled, while a frigid girl may also get put in isolation for a while.

You can see from all this that the sexual *mores* of the South Pacific islanders are anything but simple. You don't have to bother threading your way through the maze of conditions and qualifications for exile. The important point is that there *is* such an island, and at all times it's stocked with two or three hundred island girls, serving "sentences" of three months to two or three years, depending on the nature of their offense. There are no guards. None are needed. The island is well isolated by water, and even if any prisoner could escape, she wouldn't, because it would earn her eternal disgrace in her tribe.

I found out all the foregoing facts in the spring of 1949, when I was kicking around Tonga and the Fiji Islands working for Allied Tin Exports, Ltd. I picked up the story as a bit of interesting island gossip, and filed it away in the back of my head as a good anecdote to relate when and if I ever got back to the States. You know—sitting around with a beer in your hand, amus-ing the yokels by saying, "and they also tell the tale of the island of lonely women, exiled from their community for crimes of love—"

And then the story ceased to be island gossip for me, and became grim reality. We jump now to June, 1954. I wasn't in the tin business any more, having quit with a good bundle of cash and the idea of loafing for a couple of years. I was still in the South Pacific, though. I had been mixed up in a little gun-running in Indonesia, had taken part in a small uprising in the Philippines—nothing exciting, really, though it sounds adventurous as all get-out. Just a lot of mucking around in sweaty jungles. By '54 I was getting ready to call it a day and head back to civilization. And then, in New Guinea, I met this fellow who was looking for a companion on a little trip to the islands to the east.

His name was Kelly, Sean Brian Kelly, and he was an American millionaire type who wanted to cruise the islands, taking movies and I suppose having some fun with the native women. He offered me $350 a week to keep him company, and at that price I was more than willing.

He had this sloop, *Green Erin*, and he had a redhead named Donna to go with him. Kelly gave me the impression that I could share Donna with him on the trip, but sorry to say I never got the chance. I saw her only once—a tall, broad-shouldered girl with flashing eyes, flaming hair, and magnificent breasts. She was drunk, and Kelly was drunker, and when I showed up at the dock she was telling him off. He was trying to paw her, and as I showed up he grabbed hold of her and pulled her blouse open. Buttons went popping everywhere. She had nothing on underneath but skin, and what I saw made me tingle all over.

"Heresh my ol' pal Lin," he muttered drunkenly. "Take a look at her, Lin. Ain't she a beaut?"

Donna hauled off and belted Kelly, and pulled her blouse closed, in that order. Then she finished telling him off, in words that would blister the paper if I wrote them down, and stalked away.

"Come on," Kelly mumbled. "We're leaving now."

I wanted to tell him that storm warnings were up halfway across the Pacific, but he wouldn't have any of that. He was determined to strand Donna here, and he threatened to take off by himself if I wouldn't go with him. So I had no choice. The pale globes that were Donna's breasts still had my heart pounding, and I regretted the dumb quarrel that had cost us her services. Before the trip was over, though, I was wishing longingly for the chance to enter a monastery and never see a female form again.

Drunk as he was, Kelly handled that sloop pretty well. He sobered up after a while, and was bitter on the subject of women in general and Donna in particular. He vowed to take out our frustrations on the women of the first land we struck.

For a couple of days we headed eastward. We were in the vicinity of the Gilbert Islands when the gale came down on us out of the northeast. It smashed up the rigging and beat the bejabbers out of the ship, and it began to be very clear to me that *Green Erin* was going to go down. I tried to get the idea across to Kelly, but he wasn't having any. Full of Bushmill's, he struck a pose and bellowed against the winds, "This vessel can withstand a hurricane!"

"Maybe so, but it isn't going to survive this gale. Let's break the dinghy out and head to shore."

The ship was filling fast. I made my way to the radio and sent out an S.O.S., over Kelly's violent objections. Then I got the dinghy out. Kelly was drunker than ever, and refused to abandon the ship, though we were shipping water seriously now.

He was somewhere aft, roaring defiance at the elements. I went to get him, figuring I'd knock him out and stow him in the dinghy, when a wave the size of the Empire State Building hit us. I held on tight, and when the wave had passed, Kelly was gone.

Just gone. And the boat sinking. What the hell would *you* do? I don't know, but all I did was to get into the dinghy, cut loose from the sinking sloop, and head for the nearest spot of dry land.

The winds and waves helped me. Twenty minutes later, I was tossed up on the rough coral shore of a pint-sized atoll. I had seen the sloop go under minutes after I had abandoned it.

I lay face-down on the beach for maybe half an hour, with the dinghy pulled up alongside. Finally I caught my breath and felt less waterlogged. I propped myself up and looked around.

The first thing I saw was a stand of palm trees. Then I saw the women.

There were ten of them, with the dusky skin of the islander. Their jet-black hair hung in ringlets to their shoulders. Some of them were totally nude. Others wore a little fringe of beads around their hips, and a few modest souls added a necklace that did absolutely nothing to cover their full breasts. They were all young, all pretty. And me who hadn't had a woman in ten days or more. I got the idea that I had landed in paradise, sure enough.

More women appeared. Young ones, mature ones, but not old ones. Naked ones, ones wearing strings of beads, girls with wreaths of flowers around their waists. All lovely. All looking at me with gleaming eyes.

Not a single man.

There were swarms of them, now—at least forty or fifty, though who can count when surrounded by so much delicious nudity? Four of them took me by the arms, raised me to my feet, lifted me off the ground completely. Hands fought to grab hold of me. They jostled each other like New York housewives trying to get to the bargain counter at Klein's. I thought for a minute they were going to rip me apart.

They started carrying me inland, and I soon found myself in a little ramshackle village. Still no men, but more women came flooding out from all over to see me. I found it quite odd that a village should be populated exclusively by young women. No men, no children, no oldsters. My mind began to tick. I remembered, back five years, to the old salt who had told me of Luanape.

"Three hundred women, maybe. And hungry for men. I've seen men who were shipwrecked there and who managed to escape. They were never the same afterward."

I had no doubt now. This was Luanape—and I was the prisoner of these man-hungry exiled women!

I was carried into a big hut and put down on a thick reed mat carpeted with sweet-smelling hibiscus blossoms. I found myself facing a woman who by her posture and bearing was obviously the boss here.

She was perhaps thirty. She was close to six feet tall, with breasts like swelling grapefruits and legs like coppery pillars. Her sensuous, incredibly beautiful body was nude except for a wreath of flowers that rested gently on the high, rounded thrust of her bosom.

Speaking in the simple island jargon, she identified herself as Suilone—Queen of Luanape. Just what offense had caused this massive, powerful woman to be sentenced here, I never found out—but I could see that her rule was absolute.

She ordered me to stand before her.

"Strip," she boomed.

My shirt had been washed away in the sea, and my trousers were more gone than here. But I was still flustered by the order. I hesitated, and found myself getting poked in the back by the stone points of longs spears wielded by two muscular-looking damsels.

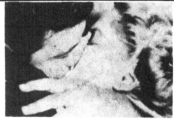
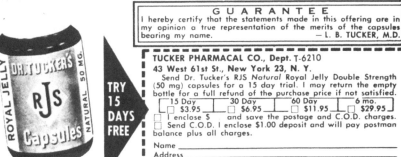

This was no time for modesty. I fumbled with my waterlogged belt, pulled it open, and stepped out of my clothing. I'm no more inhibited than the next guy, but the thought of being nude in front of an audience of about two hundred fifty women was slightly disconcerting. My ears were burning.

But they burned a little harder a minute later. Queen Suilone rose from her throne, walked with ponderous dignity to the reed mat, and lay down in front of me in a position of love. She ordered me then to satisfy her.

I was numbed. She was beautiful, lush, exciting. But how could I make love to her here—in front of this enormous crowd?

"It is—impossible," I said shamefacedly. "There are too many onlookers."

"They will stay," the queen said. "Make love to me or die."

I hesitated, and she could see plainly that I was unable at the moment to give her what she wanted. She clapped her hands and two lovelies stepped forward, bearing a bowl of some thick pinkish substance. They indicated that I should drink from it.

It was fermented coconut milk, doped with some powder ground from a native root, and if I had the formula I would be a rich man today. It was a jim-dandy aphrodisiac. After the third gulp, I felt ready to make love to a regiment of Amazons. My inhibitions dropped away. I knelt by the Queen and she drew me to her, and to the accompaniment of loud cheers from the onlookers I made love to her. She moaned like a tigress in heat, and the session lasted nearly an hour. I was sweat-soaked and exhausted when, satisfied at last, she released me.

I was immediately surrounded by a trio of tall girls who bore me off to the lagoon. There—watched carefully by the others—they gave me a thorough bath in the cool, sparkling water. I felt refreshed afterward, but I was knocked out by my bout with the ocean and my bout with Queen Suilone, and wanted nothing better than to be allowed to sleep for a week.

Some chance! Smiling lassies brought me another bowl of the coconut juice, and within half an hour I was making love again. Not to the Queen, this time, but to some of the ladies-in-waiting. I took on three in quick succession, thinking that paradise was turning out to be a pretty strenuous place. Breasts and thighs and tawny buttocks were just so much meat to me after a while.

They let me sleep—for an hour and a half. Then I was awake again, with a splitting headache and a choking sensation in my chest, and they were stuffing more of the coconut punch down my throat.

All during that night I made love—it must have been ten or twenty times. They allowed me an hour breather between each round, and kept me artificially invigorated with the coconut stuff. Even so, I grew less and less able to respond to their caresses. I was getting dizzy and incoherent. It was one long succession of soft, warm bodies hurling themselves at me.

Morning came. I was allowed to get three whole hours of sleep. Then I was awakened; my eyes were stinging, my head throbbing wildly. I was carried down to the lagoon and scrubbed again, then borne back to the Queen's hut. She greeted me with ecstatic little squeals, and wrapped her powerful arms about me, pressing me to her mighty breasts.

And so it went on, for three days. Three days of sheer torture. I've always been a healthy and virile chap, but I was prodded right to my limits. Every girl on that island wanted to rid herself of her frustrations. Except for the Queen, who had me once each day, I don't think I made love to any of them twice. By the end of it, I was like a mechanical man, a robot built for one purpose only. I couldn't think, couldn't talk, couldn't keep them away from me.

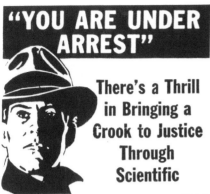
There are limits to male human endurance, no matter what the love-happy women of Luanape seemed to think. I couldn't keep up the pace forever. Early on the morning of the fourth day I passed out cold, and when I woke it was sundown. So I had been out for an entire day, at least. No doubt they were furious.

As a matter of fact, they were. I was tied down in the Queen's hut, and Suilone was standing over me with an enormous knife in her hand. I looked up in puzzlement.

"You are no longer of use to us," I was informed. "Therefore we will kill you."

I tried to explain that I could go on being of use to them, if they would only let me rest a while between stud appointments. But Suilone was determined to kill me. They had had their fun; now they were going to show their hatred for the sex that had exiled them. Her eyes ran the length of my naked body, and with a cold chill I realized that she had some particularly grisly method in mind for the execution.

I was too tightly bound to even wriggle. Suilone was whacking that blade around as if she meant immediate business, but to my surprise I learned that the grim event was to take place at sunrise.

The Luanape women danced and sang in front of me for an hour, stamping their feet, whirling about, their breasts bobbing, their bodies becoming oiled with sweat. Then, as darkness came over the island, they went to their huts, leaving me guarded by two of the oldest women.

I lay awake a long time, brooding about my fate, and finally dozed off. I was awakened in the middle of the night, by a hand jogging my shoulder.

By the moonlight I saw my two guards lying fast asleep at the mouth of the hut, and a girl of about fifteen, stark naked, was crouching at my side, efficiently sawing through my bonds. She was like a delivering angel.

"It is wrong to kill you," she murmured softly. "You must flee now, before morning, or you will die most horribly."

She helped me to my feet—I was stiff and cramped and weak as a kitten—and together we tiptoed through the quiet village and down to the beach. Her name was Arupali, she told me. She was the youngest girl on the island, sentenced because she had refused to sleep with the seventy-year-old chieftain of her tribe. And she was beautiful, though her body was still slim and boyish, and her tender breasts were but unsprouted buds as yet. She had taken pity on me, and at great personal risk had given a sleeping-drink to my guards and had cut me loose.

The dinghy was still on the beach, where I had left it. We had a tender little farewell scene—she pressed her body against me for a minute, letting me fondle her young breasts, and then she was gone, scampering up the beach, waving at me. I watched her trim little rear vanish into the underbrush, and hoped she wouldn't be blamed for my disappearance.

Then I shoved off, paddling desperately despite my state of utter exhaustion. I wondered how Queen Suilone was going to take it when I was found missing.

The rest of that day is a blank. I drifted on the calm sea, sun-crazy and thirsty, and I don't know how long I drifted. But I was picked up, finally, by a copra ship bound for Borneo, and I was in pretty bad shape when they found me.

I spent three weeks flat on my back, recuperating. My little interlude on Luanape had cost me twenty pounds, and maybe five years of my life.

But that's the story, and there's the island. If you feel hungry for feminine embrace, head Pacificward. But I warn you—you may get more than you're bargaining for, on the island of Queen Suilone. And the next time, there might not be some tender-hearted girl to help you escape.

The end

by

Jim Hollister

92

THE ARABIAN SLAVE GIRL RACKET

THE CITY WAS YANBU, on the west coast of oil-rich Saudi Arabia. The time was midday of a sleepy summer afternoon in 1958. The place was the sumptuous villa I had rented for a song a week before. I was in Saudi Arabia to gather background for an article being prepared by a national American news magazine.

I was typing up my first few days' notes when there was a discreet knock at my study door. Ahmed, my house-boy, entered timidly to announce that I had a visitor.

I had been expecting the British consul for dinner, but the time of his arrival was still several hours away. Frowning, I said, "Who wants to see me?"

(Continued on next page)

"I couldn't take my eyes off the ravishingly beatiful slave girl who was undressing in front of me at the command of her owner. Yet, I knew the whole idea of buying this voluptuous woman was utterly fantastic."

93

"Mohammed al-Kamakim," the boy murmured. And, forestalling my next question, he added, "The dealer in slaves."

I choked back my surprise. The villa had come equipped with a staff of six people when I had rented it, and I had assumed that they were employees. But now I remembered the stories I had heard about the still-flourishing slave trade of Saudi Arabia. I wanted to know more.

"Show him in," I said.

Mohammed al-Kamakim entered a few moments later. He was a short, wiry man without an ounce of superfluous flesh on his body. Beady eyes watched me closely from both sides of a hawklike beak of a nose.

He made a deep *salaam* and for two or three minutes we did nothing but exchange compliments, in the manner of the East. He carefully avoided blessing me in Allah's name, as would be customary between two Arabs, because that would have obliged me to bless him in the name of Christ—a blessing he would be forced to refuse.

When we were through with the formalities, al-Kamakim said, "You are fortunate to have rented one of the finest villas in all Yanbu. The breeze from the sea, is it not wonderful?"

Indeed it was, Yanbu is on the Red Sea, and in arid Saudi Arabia, where the ground yields oil but no water, a genuine sea breeze is something to be treasured.

He went on, "The staff of your villa is of the best. I know, for it was I who supplied them. But perhaps you would care to add to your roster of servants."

I frowned. "I'm only planning to be in Yanbu about six weeks," I said. "Then I'll be moving inland. So I wouldn't want to invest in a slave"—the words sounded as strange to my ears as they look on paper—"for any great length of time." It was like a conversation with a stockbroker, I thought.

Al-Kamakim smiled toothily. "We could arrange a short-term hire-purchase," he said. "I would re-purchase the slaves when you chose to leave Yanbu." Before I could protest, he said, "I have brought a few samples to show you, *effendi*. Will you honor me by examining them?"

My curiosity prevailed over my fundamental disgust for the whole idea, and I allowed him to show me his wares. He clapped his hands and the door opened. A magnificent Negro, perhaps six feet six inches tall and powerfully built, marched in and stood silently at attention before me.

"He is of the Sudan," al-Kamakim said. "Trained as a bodyguard and messenger. Strong, intelligent, devoted, reliable. And utterly silent. He neither reads nor writes nor speaks."

At a signal from his owner, the giant black opened his mouth. I shuddered at the discovery that the slave's tongue had been cut out!

"No," I said hurriedly. "I don't want him."

"An excellent buy, *effendi*. As loyal as a dog, and he's only $350."

"No. Sorry, not interested."

Al-Kamakim smiled faintly and dismissed the towering African. An instant later a small Arab boy with shining eyes and an impudent grin wriggled through and stood before me.

"The boy is only twelve," Al-Kamakim commented, "His services are valued highly—but he is yours for $450, and I will guarantee to buy him back at a good price when you leave Yanbu."

I shook my head forcefully. He was an attractive-looking little scamp, but I didn't need a houseboy!

"His previous owner was a great shiekh," Al-Kamakim said cajolingly.

"Maybe so. But I have a houseboy already."

"This lad is much more than a houseboy!"

"His other talents are of no interest to me," I said.

Al-Kamakim shrugged; the boy made a neat little curtsey and ran out of the room. "Perhaps my final offering will catch your eye," he said. He clapped his hands.

The door opened and a girl entered, swathed completely in the enveloping white gown of the Arab woman. Her face was veiled.

"This is Reema," the slavemaster announced. "She is sixteen, and I will stake my share of Paradise that she is untouched. Her price is $2,000 American—but you may enjoy her while you are in Yanbu, and I will guarantee to repurchase her at three quarters that price when you leave."

I stared at her, while Al-Kamakim watched me, and at the precise psychological moment he signaled Reema to remove her veil. I gasped involuntarily at her beauty. She was fair-skinned, with flawless lips and large, dark, solemn eyes. Her face was one of the loveliest I had ever seen.

While I stood frozen by her beauty, Al-Kamakim took advantage of my hesitation to remove the rest of her clothing. She stood in the middle of the heap of discarded wraps, totally nude, and I feasted my eyes. Her waist was slim, but her buttocks were full, always a valued asset for an Arabian girl. She had round, high breasts—"breasts like twin pomegranates," in the words of *The Arabian Nights*—and her hips, her thighs, her ankles were all of the most surpassing perfection. She was a gem. And as she stood there, eyes modestly downcast, lovely young breasts rising and falling quickly, I felt myself break out into a cold sweat of desire.

I told myself savagely, *Cut this crap out! You're an American, male, thirty-two years old. You were married once and you're the father of a couple of kids. Stop looking at this girl as if you want to add her to your harem.*

"T-take her away!" I stammered finally. "I don't want to see her or any other slaves! I'm not in the market for buying, you understand me? Go!"

Al-Kamakim smiled confidently. Ordering Reema to don her clothes, he said to me, "I would not wish to intrude any further on your privacy, *effendi*. But she is lovely, is she not?"

"Sure she is. So is the Taj Mahal, but I'm not going to buy that either!"

"As you wish, kind friend. But I shall withhold the girl from the market for a week, just in case you reverse your decision."

"I don't intend to."

"Perhaps not. But you need merely send your houseboy to fetch me. Farewell."

After Al-Kamakim and his troupe had departed, I hurriedly poured myself a drink to settle my shaking nerves. The sight of that beautiful naked girl had put me into a tizzy. I was furious with myself. The girl was half my age. And an Arab, too. Was I a cradle-robber? Had I come to this?

I threw myself busily into my work, and before I knew it was time for my dinner appointment with the British Consul. He turned out to be exceptionally friendly, and over cognac I told him of my experience with Al-Kamakim, in the afternoon—editing out, for the sake of modesty, the surge of desire I had felt at the sight of Reema's nakedness.

I pumped him for information about the Saudi Arabian slave trade. What he told me, I'll set down here to fill you in on the background.

Slavery in Saudi Arabia is legal—one of the few places on Earth where the trade hasn't been abolished. The Koran specifies that slavery is permissible, provided certain regulations are met. A master, according to the holy book, has to treat his slave humanely, feeding him and clothing him well. The master must also assume responsibility for all slave children. After seven years, a slave can demand his freedom and get it, but few do, since the only life they know is slavery. However, several of the important members of King Saud's cabinet are said to have risen out of slavery to their high rank.

The number of slaves in Saudi Arabia is unknown, despite separate investigations by the British, the French, and the U.N. The Saudi Arabian government takes a dim view of such probing in its internal affairs. Nevertheless, at least half a million slaves are in bondage there, and perhaps as many as a million. Slave traders are licensed.

The center of the trade is Mecca, the holy city. Here, open trading is common, though really desirable slaves are sold through private showings of the kind Al-Kamakim had staged for me. Young virgins get the highest prices, with old women the least costly, at around $100.

Many of the slaves enter from Yemen, at the lower end of the Red Sea coast. The Yemeni slavers raid villages and carry off likely prospects; but not all slaves are obtained through raids, since sometimes impoverished farmers will peddle their extra daughters in return for a few sacks of grain.

Another big source of slaves is Africa, as always. Ethiopia and the Sudan supply most of the market. Natives are rounded up at gunpoint in the jungle and are driven to the Red Sea, where they are ferried across into Arabia in old landing-craft left over from the days of Rommel's Afrika Korps. Another possible route is overland by camel caravan to the Gulf of Aden, where the Red Sea is at its narrowest.

My consular informant added, "A British report to UNESCO a couple of years ago turned up the interesting fact that a great many Moslem Africans are duped into buying what they think is a pilgrimage to Mecca—but it's a one-way ticket to slavery that they've really purchased!"

Many former Nazis, left in Africa at the smashing of Rommel's army, are happily engaged as slave-runners now. Theoretically, it's been against the law since 1936 to bring new slaves to Saudi Arabia, unless they had already been slaves in the country from which they were brought. From time to time Saudi officials will stop a slave caravan to perform a cynical check on the status of the merchandise, but standard bribes are handed over, and no complications ensue. Frequently the border authorities themselves are engaged in the traffic.

I listened to all this—and to some grisly tales of how eunuchs are manufactured for the still-thriving market in harem guards—and my blood ran a little colder at the thought that such things were still going on in twentieth-century times. The shiekhs drive around in air-conditioned Cadillacs now, but the old evil practices

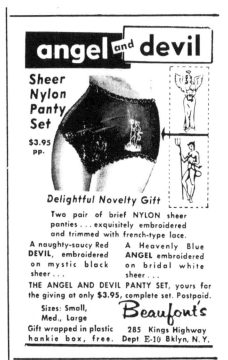

96

of the East are far from dead.

For the next three days I worked steadily, staying indoors to avoid the heat. My mind wandered continually to the image of Reema. Al-Kamakim was holding her for a week, I kept reminding myself. After that, she might vanish into the harem of some multimillionaire cousin of King Saud. A dozen times I was tempted to send Ahmed out to fetch Al-Kamakim, and a dozen times I stifled the impulse. At night, Reema seemed to hover around my bed in my dreams. I gritted my teeth, told myself that I wasn't going to get personally involved in this filthy traffic in human flesh.

On the fourth day, Al-Kamakim and Reema paid me a visit, uninvited.

"I have had an offer for Reema," he said. "At the beginning of next week, she goes to a harem in Medina. Her purchaser is sixty years old, and fond of virgins."

"*No!*" I bellowed involuntarily.

"No? You find the thought unpleasant?"

I clenched my fists. $2,000 was a lot of money, but I was getting a lot more for the work I was doing here. Ideas flitted through my head. If I bought Reema, kept her here without touching her, and gave her her freedom—it would cost me a pile, but it would be a genuinely good deed.

Al-Kamakim saw me wavering, and hammered home his sales-pitch. Within an hour, the deal was struck. I bargained him down a little—Reema was mine for $1,750, and when I left Yanbu he would take her back for $1,200—the difference representing the value of her virginity, which he assumed I would take, as well as her use for five weeks.

He accompanied me to the bank while I had my check certified. The teller looked at me strangely, as though reading my mind. I couldn't look him in the eye. *I've just bought a slave girl*, I thought wonderingly.

Alone in my study with Reema, I smiled at her to get rid of my own nervousness. She was swathed from head to toe in cotton, but I knew what lay underneath the robes.

"How old are you?" I asked.

"Fifteen."

Younger than I thought. I nibbled my lip. "Where were you born?"

"Hadiyah. My mother was of a shiekh's harem."

"You were born into slavery, then?"

"Yes."

"How have you managed to remain a virgin for fifteen years, then?" I asked.

"I lived in the harem until I was thirteen. I was betrothed to the shiekh, but he was very old and never summoned me. When he died, one of the harem eunuchs stole me and kept me a year, till I was old enough to fetch a good price. Al-Kamakim bought me from him last year, and has kept me ever since."

It sounded like a story out of Haroun Al-Raschid's days. But it was a tale of the twentieth century, I reminded myself.

"Will you do away with my maidenhood tonight?" she asked softly.

I shook my head. "I'm not going to touch you at all, Reema. You'll live here with me in your own room. When I leave Yanbu, I'm going to give you your freedom."

To my surprise, she began to sob. She did not want freedom, she explained; she had been trained for harem life, and if I abandoned her she would fall into prostitution or else be recaptured and peddled by some other slave trader. "You are good and kind," she murmured. "I will stay with you always, as your concubine." I tried to inform her that in a few months I would go back to America, where concubines are frowned upon, but America seemed as remote to her as Mars. She pleaded with me not to free her.

Suddenly she began to remove her robes. I protested, but to no effect; she was a woman, with all of woman's wiles. When she had stripped down to mere filmy underthings that covered her hips and breasts, she began to dance. Perhaps it was a harem dance, perhaps just some improvised bumps and grinds. But it left me drenched with sweat. My heart thundered; I lost control of myself, and as she ripped away the final bits of gauze, I pulled her body against mine.

She drew me down to the couch, and her body writhed with the inherited arts of thousands of years, she had been well trained in all, and her performance was incredible. My hands cupped breasts as tender as a baby's skin.

Guilt flooded in on me when it was over. Reema was smiling radiantly in glow of her first fulfillment as a woman, but all I could think was that I had taken this slave girl. I felt sick and disgusted with myself.

Reema danced again, raising my spirits. And, later, we made love, and she was even more of a virtuoso with her body than the last time.

Reema remained with me all my time in Yanbu, though I took care to keep her out of sight when my few European acquaintances came calling. Shortly before my departure, Al-Kamakim paid me a visit, asked if I were satisfied, and wanted to know whether I still planned to sell Reema back to him.

I struggled against my conscience for a while, trying to devise some insane plan to bring her back to America with me. But at last I gave in, and sold her back to the trader for the agreed price. I was miserable when she left; she, in her turn, kissed me lightly, and murmured, "I will always be grateful to you, my American!"

So there it is. For $550, Reema was mine a little over a month. I learned later that she had been sold to one of Saudi Arabia's most powerful princes, and now was a chief wife of considerable importance. It was a strange experience in my life, and half the time today I tell myself that I should never have become mixed up in the slave traffic to such an extent. But the other half of the time, I remember the feel of Reema's tender body against my own, and I envy the lucky shiekh whose harem she now ornaments.

The end

A TEMPORARY HUSBAND IN LADAKH

by
Karl-Heinz Kirschner

ALTHOUGH the name of Tibet is now splashed across the headlined pages of every newspaper, thanks to the brutal suppression of Tibetan liberty by the forces of Mao Tse-tung, far less is heard of Tibet's neighbor on the roof of the world—Ladakh, the so-called "Little Tibet," where women have many husbands.

I visited Ladakh in 1955, travelling alone, en route to Tibet itself. As a citizen of West Germany, I was able to acquire visas to enter lands that are closed to Americans.

Ladakh is in the eastern part of the State of Jammu and Kashmir. Politically, it is claimed both by India and Pakistan, in a dispute that is more than ten years old and shows no sign of ending. But the true affiliation of Ladakh is not with India but with its eastern neighbor, Tibet. It shares with Tibet not only religion, but blood, dress, language, and custom. Mongols, Buddhists, the people of Ladakh and those of Tibet both inhabit cold, lofty wastelands. Even in the days before Red Chinese oppression, it was next to impossible for a Westerner to get into Tibet. Ladakh, though, is accessible to all, even now.

(Continued on next page)

It is truly unfortunate that the Chinese Communists have taken over Tibet if only for the reason that the generous natives of that primitive land will certainly not be as hospitable to visitors as they were before.

A TEMPORARY HUSBAND IN LADAKH

(Continued from page 99)

I set out on horseback early in August, 1955, departing from Srinagar, the capital of Kashmir. My goal was to cross the towering heights of Ladakh and Tibet alone, enter into the forbidden land, and take films. I did not know, as I set out that night, that I was destined to become the husband-for-a-night of a beautiful young woman of Ladakh.

Strapped to the saddle of my sturdy beast were bags containing blankets, a collapsible tent, and my cameras. I also had many silver rupees with me. I was carrying little food, hoping to depend on the mercies of the people as I travelled.

My itinerary was north to Gandarbal, then east through the Sind Valley to Sonamarg, and on to Leh, the capital of Ladakh, and thence to forbidden Tibet. At the end of my first day I had reached Woyil Bridge, where I camped by the edge of the Sind River. The great suspension bridge crossed rapid, snow-flecked water.

From there I moved on the next day, through flower-filled meadows, magically green valleys, following the Sind. Only 8,000 feet above sea level, the scenery was incredibly lovely. At Sonamarg, "the golden meadow," the pastures were dotted with silvery birch trees and colorful wildflowers. An array of massive glaciers looked down from the distant heights.

Going on to Baltal, though, the climate began to change. Crossing the Zoji Pass, at an altitude of 11,580 feet, I entered onto the road that leads eastward to Tibet.

The trail became difficult—snow, sleet, high winds all assailed me. I had entered a strange, lofty plateau on which nothing grew. Not a tree anywhere, hardly any grass, not a single flower. I spent a savagely cold night at Matayan, huddled in my tent with only my horse for warmth, cursing myself for having gone out into these wastelands alone.

In the morning the weather was better, and I moved on. The next stop was Dras, the land of the Balti people. These tough, hard-working Slavs are marooned six months out of the year by snow. Next came Karghil, the halfway point, where a steady rain caused landslides and made the going treacherous. I was now in the heart of Ladakh, the beginning of the Himalaya country.

Mulbekh marked the beginning of the pure Tibetan-type country. I followed along the pony track, pausing at whitewashed villages to purchase food—powdered barley mixed with hot tea, salt, and rancid butter. Tibetans in their flowing woolen coats and embroidered boots watched me in curiosity, and asked if I planned to go on beyond the vague Ladakh–Tibet border into the forbidden land itself.

It was the height of summer, yet the temperature rarely rose higher than 30 degrees. The land was barren, with scattered oases of irrigated land. Vast stony mountains bordered the plateau. It was a weird landscape, looking like someplace of Mars.

So far the trip had certainly had its discomforts, but there had been no real difficulties—that is, I had suffered no injuries nor any illness. But my luck began to change. I had passed through the city of Leh, which is the metropolis of Ladakh with a population of about 3,000, and I was steadily plodding across the Himalayas to the Tibetan border, when I began to detect in myself the symptoms of fever.

It came up slowly—a throbbing in my head, a buzzing in my ears. I attributed it to the high altitude and the thin air. But my face began to feel flushed and my stomach was uncertain. I realized that I was getting sick—far from any outpost of western civilization.

Still, I refused to turn back. I crossed through Chang Pass, which breasts the mighty Himalayas at 18,000 feet above sea level. My route would take me through the village of Tankse, and then on to Tibet. But I was still some miles from Tankse when the fever struck in all its force. I had to dismount, lest I fall from my horse and injure myself.

I searched the gray distances. And there, against the leaden sky, I saw outlined the squat, dumpy shape of a good-sized Ladakhi dwelling.

Weakly, I tottered toward it, with my horse following obediently behind me. Every step was agony. Some mountain-dwelling bacterium had no doubt entered my body at my last stop, and now I was in its grip. I had visions of myself dying here, in these lonely, wind-swept wastes, and being cast into an unmarked grave without a Christian prayer to be said for me.

I reached the house. A tall Ladakhi man appeared in the doorway. He wore his hair in pigtails, and above his trousers, which were tight at the ankles, he had draped a long home-spun robe girded at the middle with a purple belt. Weird, alien though he was, to me he was a sign of humanity.

In a hoarse voice I muttered, using the Tibetan dialect I had learned, "I am a traveler… I come from Srinigar… I am sick…"

And then I staggered forward and fell to the frozen earth.

My Ladakhi savior scooped me up and carried me, none too gently, into his house. After a few minutes inside, I began to revive.

I was in a combined parlor-dining room. Soup was simmering on a stove, bringing moisture to my lips. The room was clouded with the thick smoke of *argol,* the dried cow-dung that is the universal fuel in these regions where wood is so scarce. There was a hole in the roof, through which some of the smoke escaped, and through which a minute quantity of light and fresh air was able to enter. The atmosphere was heavy and warm, which was just what I wanted after my long fever-wracked trip through the thin, cold wastelands.

I was placed on a thick rug, while the inhabitants of the house bustled around me, as excited to have a guest from the outside world as I was to have found a place where I could rest.

"Soup is almost ready," I was informed by the mistress of the house. She was a young woman, no more than twenty-five. Her body was hidden by the shapeless garments that she wore, but the features of her face were delicate and finely formed.

The other inhabitants of the house included three men and a small girl. The three men were brawny and had a strong family resemblance. The child, who was about three, was naked, as if in defiance of the whistling winds outside.

From what I knew of Ladakhi ways, I understood immediately the truth of the situation. Ladakh is a land where the women are greatly outnumbered by the men. As a result, each woman is allowed to marry as many as three husbands. When she marries, she customarily takes on as minor husbands two of the younger brothers of the bridegroom. Superfluous males go off to the populous Buddhist monasteries.

This was just such an arrangement. The male who had carried me in from outside was the oldest of the three brothers, and the chief husband. The two younger men were also husbands of the slim young woman. Which one of the three was the father of the little girl I never knew, nor do I think there is any way of finding out such information definitely. The girl addressed all three of her mother's husbands as "uncle."

The arrangement seemed to work. To cheer me up, the three husbands told jokes, which I found incomprehensible—and they laughed uproariously at each other's jokes. At last the soup

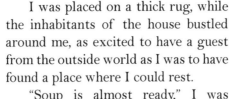

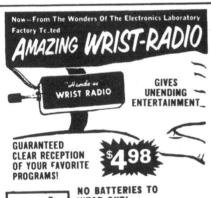

was ready. The youngest of the three husbands fed me the thick, warm soup. Gobs of fat floated in it, and unidentified chunks of meat, but so hungry and cold was I that I would have accepted anything at all with gratitude.

Following the soup, the main course was served—tea and *tsamba*. The tea was poured into a bamboo churn, together with a lump of rancid yak butter and salt. The *tsamba*, a parched ground barley, was shaped into balls and dunked into the bitter tea. This is the standard diet throughout Ladakh and Tibet.

I ate slowly, feeling my fever still on the rise. Through the dining room's open door I could see a small bedroom, with a narrow bed. I knew that the wife slept there, with her chosen spouse of the night. The other two brothers would unroll blankets and sleep on the living-room floor.

The head of the household was very definitely the wife. I could see that her husbands obeyed her every command. Probably her prestige was even higher because she had mothered a girl child, such a rarity in Ladakh.

My fever grew rapidly worse as the evening progressed, and I knew I was becoming delirious. My hosts were very perturbed by this worsening of my condition. As is true throughout most of the orient, hospitality is raised almost to a sacred obligation, and it would be most unfortunate for them if I happened to die while in their care. I heard them discussing the situation, and finally two of the brothers lifted me in their powerful arms and carried me into the bedroom.

Feebly I protested, knowing that the one bed of the house was being sacrificed to me, but they paid no attention. They undressed me, having a little difficulty with my Western-style clothes, and when I was completely undressed they placed me in the bed, covering me with layer after layer of thick, warm quilted blankets.

There I lay for many hours, unable to sleep, moaning in my pain. Much later in the night, one of the brothers came to me with a bowl of soup, and fed it to me by holding the rim of the bowl to my mouth while I sipped. I felt somewhat better, but the fever had not abated, and sleep was impossible.

Perhaps an hour passed. Then the door of my bedroom opened again, and a slim figure entered, carrying a lamp. I opened my eyes and perceived that it was the young wife.

She set the lamp down on the crude table adjoining the bed, and said softly, "Are you awake?"

"Yes."

"Are you in pain?"

"I am very sick," I told her, groping for the words.

"I will take your sickness away," she said.

I watched her through slitted lids. To my bewilderment, she proceeded to open the belt of the bulky gown she was wearing. Within moments, she had peeled it away and she stood nude before me.

I had never suspected, from looking at her in her shapeless garments, that she could be so lovely. Her elfin body was perfectly formed, with small, high, tip-tilted breasts, curving hips, delicious thighs. The light flickered over her coppery skin.

I could not have been in a less responsive mood. I was sick, I was weary, and I was a guest in the house. Furthermore, I had never expected to have such intimate contact with people of Ladakh.

I muttered, "No … you mustn't … it is not right to do this …"

She smiled, showing flawless white teeth. "My husbands do not mind. Tonight you will be my husband, since you are sleeping in my bed."

And she slipped under the blankets next to me.

She pressed her body for its

"He'll see me!"

full length against mine, and the touch of her cool skin against my fever-consumed body was like ice. I was too weak to respond. Her arms went around my body, and she took my hands and placed them on the little perfect globes of her breasts.

I don't know how long she remained. I was half asleep, half delirious from fever. But gradually—as though she were drawing the fever out of my body—I began to feel less ill. My natural masculine instincts began to assert themselves. I became more active; and together we loved in a strange, dreamlike way, the entire experience seeming totally unreal.

I was not aware of the borderline between wakefulness and sleep. Perhaps I dozed off the moment after the consummation. In any event, almost immediately it was dawn, and I was awake, and the girl at my side awoke also, sitting up and letting the blankets slide off her.

"How do you feel?" she asked.

"Fine," I said.

And it was true. I was ravenously hungry, and there was no hint of fever. My illness had broken during the night, and aside from a certain weakness that still lingered, I was as good as ever.

Showing no shame whatever, my hostess helped me on with my garments, still nude herself. Her daughter toddled in to observe the process.

"New uncle," the child commented.

Her mother laughed. "Yes. But he will be leaving us soon."

After we were both dressed, we entered the other part of the house. I discovered all three brothers awake, and a meal in preparation. My horse had already been fed and watered.

After a meal—tea and *tsamba*, of course—I persuaded them that I was well enough to leave. They protested, asking me to stay with them again for another night. The bed, they insisted, was mine for as long as I cared to use it. And the woman went with the bed.

The prospect was delightful, but I refused. I was well enough to continue onward, and I knew it would be a grave imposition on these men, each of whom who could only enjoy his wife's embrace every third day at best. I thanked them profusely, but they refused my offer of rupees to pay for my night's lodging.

I rode off—and, without further incident, I reached the borders of Tibet and passed over into what was then still the land of the Dalai Lama. Soon I will describe my adventures in that strange country.

Probably never again will I be a husband for a night—nor will my partner in love be so skilled, and her husbands so agreeable. The marvelous beauty of that many-husbanded girl with the delicate breasts and slim thighs will linger in my mind forever.

The end

103

Amazed, the youthful American stood transfixed, as if in a dream, while the doctor showed him the wild and snaring wolf-girl of India.

WOLF CHILDREN OF INDIA

by

Ronald Bradman

SEVERAL YEARS AGO—it was the beginning of February, 1957—I happened to be assigned to diplomatic duty in New Delhi, India. I was travelling through the province of Uttar Pradesh on official business when I received a telephone call from a friend in Lucknow.

"They've found another wolf girl," he told me. "You really ought to take a day off and come see her. It's a fantastic thing—straight out of Kipling!"

Three days later, I was being shown into an office at the Gandhi Memorial Hospital in Lucknow, in the company of my friend and several doctors. The doctor in charge of the girl, Dr. Chandra Bhose, smiled nervously at me and said, "I'm afraid you're going to be in for a bit of a shock. What you're going to see isn't pretty. Are you sure you don't want to change your mind?"

"Now that I've come this far, Dr. Bhose, I'm not going to be frightened away!"

"Very well."

He opened the door.

The sight before us was incredible. A girl of perhaps fifteen, totally nude, crouched on the floor of the office behind a barrier of stout steel mesh. Her body was fully developed, with swelling young breasts and long, lean thighs and legs.

There were two platters on the floor, one of meat, one of milk. As we entered, the wolf-girl was crouched on the floor, lapping up the milk! But she looked up at us. For an instant I peered into two steel-gray eyes devoid of any trace of humanity. They were animal's eyes—and the low growl that issued from the girl's body was the growl of a wolf!

I glanced away in confusion. Physically, she had the handsome body of a beautiful young girl. But her mind was the mind of a wolf.

"We've tried putting clothing on her," Dr. Bhose explained apologetically. "But she tears it off every time. Finally we simply decided it would be

(Continued on next page)

easier both on the girl and on us if we allowed her to remain unclad, for the time being."

My eyes returned to that slim, chocolate-skinned body, to the firm young breasts, the slim flanks. This was a girl who should be just entering womanhood, not snarling like a caged beast.

"Amazing," I muttered. "Where was she found?"

I soon learned as much as the others. The girl had been discovered a week before by two big game hunters wandering in the jungles near Lucknow. She had attempted to escape, but they had overcome her and pinioned her with rope. This was the second time in the past ten years that such an animal-child had been found near Lucknow, the other being a twelve-year-old boy discovered in 1950.

The girl walked naturally on all fours, in a kind of frog-like squat. Any attempt to stand caused her extreme discomfort, and required great effort. "She does not remain on her hind legs—excuse me, her legs—any longer than four-legged beasts normally will. The moment we release her, she sinks down into the animal posture once again."

She understood no language, and there was no glint of human intelligence in her eyes. She lapped milk without embarrassment, and devoured meat wolfishly, chewing the bones like a dog. When cooked meat was offered to her, she would indignantly refuse it, spitting at it or overturning the platter.

I was fascinated by the story. Everyone knows of Rudyard Kipling's Mowgli, in *The Jungle Book*, raised by wolves—and the ancient Roman tale of Romulus and Remus is equally familiar. But it had never occurred

to me that such occurrences were anything but fictitious—until I saw the wolf-girl of Lucknow, crouching naked in her own filth, snarling her defiance at the human beings who had plucked her from her jungle.

The smell in the room was overpowering, and the sheer animalism of the girl behind the protective barrier disturbed me greatly. I soon excused myself, and left the hospital.

The idea of a child growing to adolescence in the jungle remained with me, though, and when I returned to New Delhi several weeks later I spent an afternoon in the library, discovering whatever information I could about wolf-children of the past.

There were a good many cases reported. In almost all of them, it had been wolves who appeared to be the foster parents. Aside from the Lucknow boy of 1950, who had since died, I found a celebrated case from 1927—the Miawana wolf-boy.

On July 7 of that year, a wild boy had been found in a wolf den near the village of Miawana, some seventy-five miles from Allahabad. He was about seven or eight, and though he was capable of standing upright and walking, he preferred to crawl on his hands and knees, moving with astonishing speed. He could not speak, but barked and yipped at his captors. For several months he was studied at the Allahabad hospital; it was eventually decided that he could never be civilized, and he was placed in a mental institution, where he died soon afterward.

In 1937, a wild nine-year-old girl was discovered in Turkey, and brought to an Istanbul hospital. She had been found nude, sunning herself before a cave near the Uludagh River. She growled at her finders like a bear, fled into the cave, and was dragged forth only with great difficulty. In the hospital, a couple identified her as their daughter, carried away eight years before by a bear.

The earliest case of an animal child I found dated from 1799, in Aveyron, France. After exterminating a wolf pack that had been terrorizing

the community, the townsmen found an 11-year-old boy, naked and grimy, in the den. His nails were like claws, his body scarred from frequent violent encounters with his denmates. He was taken into the home of an Aveyron doctor, who succeeded in teaching the boy to dress himself, to eat cooked food, and to tolerate human company. But the only word he ever mastered was "eat." He died at 30.

In 1850, a two or three year old boy was found near Chandour, India, by English soldiers. He refused to wear clothes, shunned human company, never smiled or laughed or spoke. Often he would share his food with stray jackals or dogs. He died after a few months.

In 1867, another such find was made in the jungles of Bulandshahr. This time the boy, who was seven when found, lived thirty years in captivity, never learning to speak or to wear clothes. He learned to walk upright, though with difficulty, and persisted in eating his food off the ground.

Two wolf-children were found at once in 1920, near the village of Godamuri. They were both girls, one about seven, the other about two, found in a wolf-den. They were found and raised by a clergyman, Rev. Singh, who named the older one Kamala, the younger Amala. They were incapable of human sound, and their knees, elbows, soles, and palms were covered with thick callouses.

According to Rev. Singh's account, the girls slept all day, huddled together like beasts, but awoke and roamed about at night. Frequently they would call to each other in sharp barks. When clothing was given to them, they tore it to shreds.

They ate raw meat only, gnawing happily on the bones for hours. They would pounce on and devour anything that looked edible, even chickens and small livestock.

Amala died after eleven months in captivity. For two days, the older girl sulked and refused to eat. It was five years before she learned to smile, laugh, and cry.

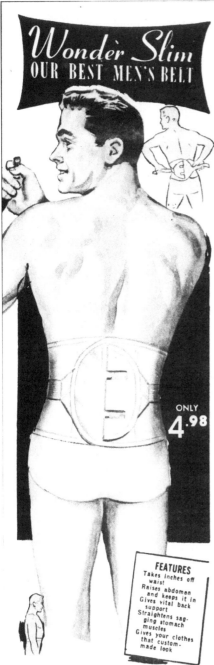
Gradually she took on some of the attributes of civilization. In 1925, she ate salt for the first time. The next year, when she was about thirteen, she permitted herself to be dressed, showing a liking for vivid red garments. Physical therapy developed her leg muscles and enabled her to walk and sit in chairs.

By the time she was fifteen, most of her animal traits had vanished, and this was evidenced by the changed attitude toward her of dogs and other animals. They no longer regarded her as one of themselves. She learned to speak, haltingly, but her vocabulary never exceeded thirty words. She learned to call several people by name, and to take part in simple games. But at eighteen, having ripened into a beautiful though mindless woman, she suddenly died. It was, perhaps, pure coincidence that eighteen years is the usual life expectancy of wolves.

These stories, and several other similar ones that I encountered, made me all the more interested in the case of the Lucknow wolf-girl. I corresponded with Dr. Bhose during the next few months, and kept in touch with the developments.

"She has been with us three months now," Dr. Bhose wrote me from Lucknow in May 1957, *"but civilization has not yet made the slightest mark on her. She has developed no modesty, nor will she eat cooked food. In all ways, she follows the classic cases of jungle children you have described to me. She does not recognize familiar faces, and she neither smiles nor laughs."*

A month later he wrote to me, *"We have been engaged in an exercise program that has very much strengthened the muscles of her legs. She is now capable of walking upright without effort, but after several days of upright posture she relapsed to the crouch. She has gained consider-*

able weight in the hospital, and no longer seems underweight. Her body has filled out, and she is in every way a beautiful young woman. Since she refuses to wear clothes and destroys every garment we give her, this causes us certain embarrassment, as you can well understand. The sight of an attractive nude girl being taken for a walk through the corridors of the hospital would tend to disturb patient discipline more than a little, of course. So until we can teach her to wear clothing, we must confine her to her quarters."

With that letter, he enclosed a photograph of her. It showed a comely teenage girl, with well-developed breasts and a sleek, desirable body. They had managed to groom her hair, which had been wild and unkept when I saw her, and she looked quite presentable, aside from the sullen expression

of her face and the animal-like glare of her eyes. Although the past case histories I had uncovered should have discouraged me, I allowed myself to hope that perhaps the wolf-girl would someday take her place in society.

A number of months went by, until it was March of 1958, and I had not heard from Dr. Bhose most of that time. Diplomatic affairs kept me busy, though now and then I wondered what was happening with the Lucknow wolf-girl.

As it developed, I was sent to Uttar Pradesh again in April 1958, and I stopped in at the Gandhi Memorial Hospital to visit Dr. Bhose. I had high hopes of seeing the girl dressed and civilized.

But these hopes were dashed promptly. Dr. Bhose came to greet me, his face sad and bleak.

"I have not had the heart to write you in many months, my friend," he said.

"Has something happened to the girl?"

"She is dead," the doctor said.

"*Dead!*" It was a shock, even though I knew that many of the past jungle children had not lived long in captivity. "Some disease—?"

"No," the doctor said, shaking his head sadly, "It is most shocking. The girl died in childbirth, sad to relate."

"But that's impossible!" I burst out. "How could she have become pregnant? She—"

"She was an attractive girl, and she spent her days in constant nudity. Many of the young hospital orderlies had access to her room. Some of them were quite ignorant. They were attracted by the girl's body; the fact that she had the mind of an animal did not seem to matter to them. Four months ago, we apprehended one of our orderlies with her."

"Disgusting!" I exclaimed.

The doctor smiled unhappily. "It was extremely shocking to us. There was some talk of sending them to prison on a rape charge, but we decided the publicity to the hospital

would be unfavorable. There was also the additional legal question."

"And the girl was pregnant?" I asked.

"Yes. She was well along. We did our best to care for her, but it was difficult. Last month she was taken prematurely. Our most skilled surgeons handled the case, but we were unable to save the mother. The strain of labor was too much for her."

"And the child?"

Dr. Bhose's lean face brightened immediately. "Yes, the child! Come with me, won't you?"

He led me through the hospital, into a ward filled with cribs and squalling infants. He picked one baby up and showed it to me. It was a girl, four or five weeks old, already equipped with a loud voice.

"This is the child," Dr. Bhose said. "One of our young doctors here is making adoption arrangements for the baby."

I looked down at the smiling, raucous infant. She looked like any other happy baby, motherless though she was. There was nothing of the beast about her. She was born with no taint of the wolf.

"The episode had its unpleasant side for us," Dr. Bhose said. "I never expected the shocking behavior that took place. But I can understand the temptation the wolf-girl must have been to those poor ignorant devils. She was beautiful, after all. A beautiful woman, flaunting her body provocatively."

"She was certainly beautiful," I agreed.

Dr. Bhose replaced the baby in the crib. "We could never have reclaimed her for civilization," he said. "No matter how long we taught her, we would probably have never instilled in her the rudiments of humanity. But now, at least, we have snatched a life from the jungle. The wolf-girl's daughter will be as lovely as her mother—and she will be a normal human being besides."

The end

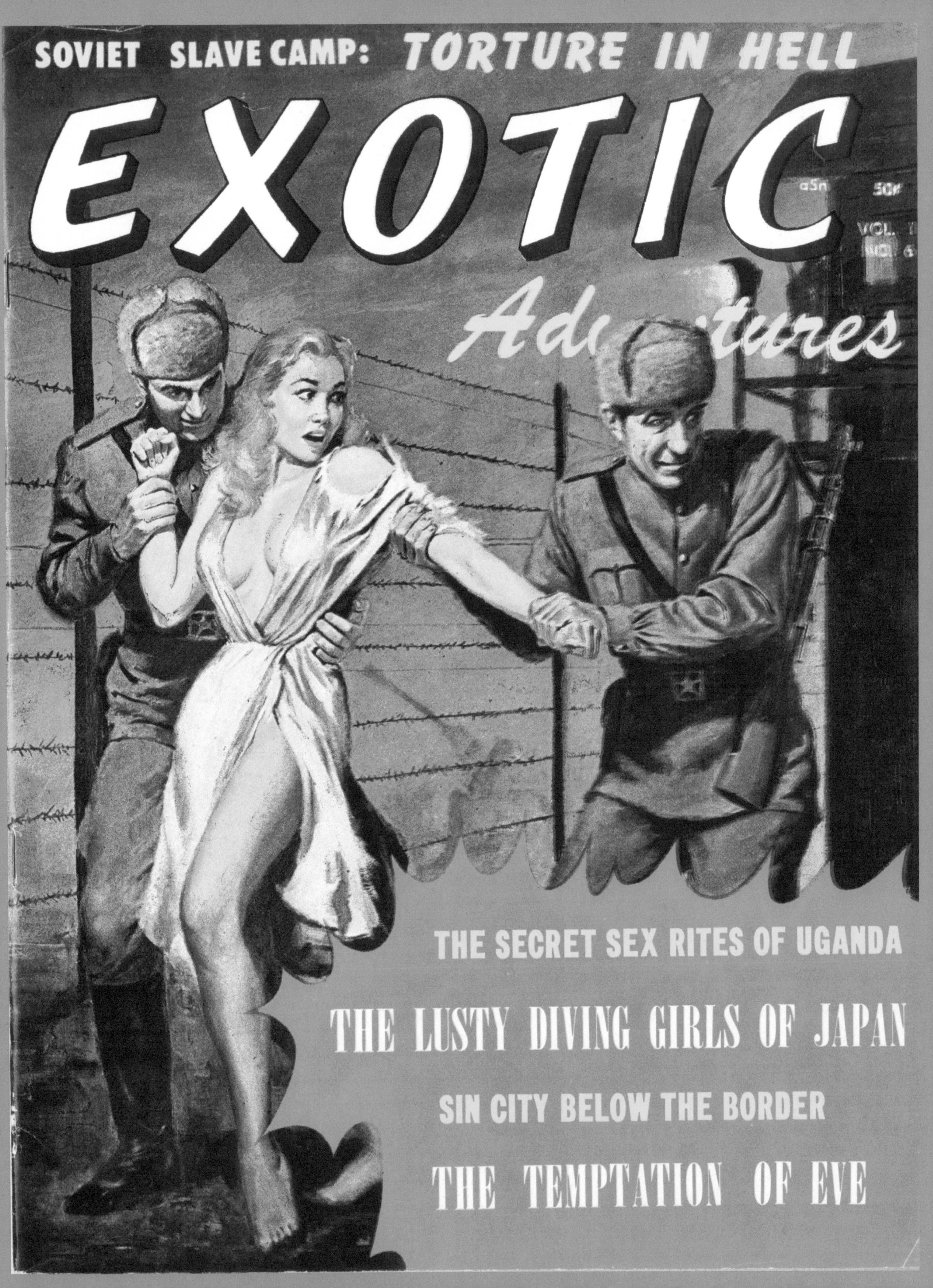
SOVIET SLAVE CAMP: TORTURE IN HELL
EXOTIC
THE SECRET SEX RITES OF UGANDA
THE LUSTY DIVING GIRLS OF JAPAN
SIN CITY BELOW THE BORDER
THE TEMPTATION OF EVE

They were about to witness what few white men had ever seen in their lives. And the only question in this mind was: "Is it worth the risk?"

I WATCHED THE SECRET SEX RITES OF UGANDA

by

Richard Banham

THE DRUMS were beating sensuously in ground-shaking rhythm. I watched, my eyes wide with astonishment, as the row of brown-skinned girls dropped their one garment and danced forward toward the waiting men. Back, forth, back, forth, in pattern of erotic action handed down from generation to generation in this little-known region of the British colony of Uganda, East Africa. In only another moment, the culmination of this incredible dance would take place right before my eyes.

My stomach was knotted with tension. Beside me, watching calmly, stood my old friends Geoffrey Niles, who had brought me here, to this wild and virtually unexplored region of Uganda, to watch the tribal sex dance, the forbidden *ugala*.

Niles smiled casually. "Ever see anything like this back in the States?"

"Are you kidding?"

(Continued on next page)

He chuckled. "The best is yet to come. Just keep watching."

Two weeks earlier I had met Niles in Entebbe, the capital of Uganda. I was on my way through East Africa on the tail end of a survey tour for the engineering firm that employs me; I had been out looking over some property in Kenya, and after making my estimate I had wangled things so I could have a few weeks of vacation before returning to the States. I was in Uganda after crossing huge Lake Tanganyika, and there I ran into Niles, who had been a wartime buddy of mine.

Niles is a lanky Englishman, about six feet six or so, and one of the coolest men who walks this earth. He pressed.

He smiled. "They're called the *ugala*. Remarkable bloody show, you know. It's a fertility dance staged this time every year. Every woman who hasn't born a child in the past year takes part. The idea is that after all the dancing there's an orgy, and the women are had by the men—no woman by her own husband. Quite a clever notion, of course. Increases the population tremendously by rematching couples of low fertility. They don't explain it that way, of course—they have some mumbo-jumbo instead—but the effect is to make a lot of babies."

I moistened my lips nervously. "You've seen this dance, you say?"

"Oh, yes. Rather a shocker, too."

"Right. We leave on Monday."

And on Monday we left. Geoff had provided a Land Rover for us, and he drove it himself, explaining that on a trip such as this he didn't think it was wise either to use a native driver or one of the British ones. This would be a highly unofficial two-man expedition. "I'll have to ask you not to take any pictures of the dance, either," he said. "The natives think you're stealing their souls with your camera."

I agreed, and we set off, heading northward from Entebbe. The road was excellently paved, though narrow and twisting, and Geoff drove confidently.

Uganda is small, as African countries go, but it contains a wild profusion of scenery—lovely silver lakes and giant volcanoes, deep craters, towering bamboo forests and grass higher than your head. On our trip northward to the wild country I saw snow-topped mountains looming

pumped my hand warmly, though, and told me he was employed in the British diplomatic service in Uganda, which has been having some troublesome problems with rebellious tribesmen.

That night, as we sat on a veranda virtually at lakeside, sipping gimlets and looking out over the lake, Niles told me about the secret sex dances.

"I was up there last year to have a look," he said. "Quite unbelievable, old man. They're staged in the north, up near the border. Pretty wild country, you know—the Karamojong roam there, and they used to be head-hunters.

Still are, if you believe some of the stories you hear."

"What about these dances?" I

"And the natives don't mind you watching?"

"As long as the onlookers don't interfere."

I nodded, and took a deep gulp of my drink. I was tremendously anxious to see the festivities first-hand, but it was a little awkward for me to say what was really on my mind.

Geoffrey, bless him, seemed to be telepathic. He said lazily, "D'ye think you'd be interested in going up there for a look?"

"Alone?"

"Of course not. I'd go with you." "Well, I wouldn't want to inconvenience you—

"Don't be silly, man. This is an experience you'll never forget. And you'll never see its like anywhere else in the world."

"Well—"

"We'll leave next Monday. Will that be convenient for you?"

I grinned broadly. "Damned right it will."

"One favor, though."

"Of course," I said.

"Don't let anyone else know where you're going. The British government is trying to stamp out these dances, y'see. And it would be damned awkward for me if word got around that a British official was making little trips up to watch them."

Of course, Geoff. I'll keep mum."

in the distance, and I also sweltered in the heat, since Uganda is right on the Equator.

Although the natives in the Entebbe area are fairly westernized, they began to seem more primitive as we went further from civilization. It became a common sight to see native girls striding along the road wearing only a waist-band of leaves, or sometimes merely a string of beads around the hips. The most usual garment, though, was the *futu*—a coarse square of cloth that covered the body from the shoulders to the thighs. The *futus* were loose garments held by a knot at the left shoulder. This left the right breast exposed, but this was hardly a startling sight in Africa, where native women rarely wear anything above their waists except in those regions where the European influence has been particularly strong.

"How did you find out about these ceremonies?" I asked.

"Word travels. I have many friends among the natives. They know I'm interested in studying the native ways."

Geoffrey chuckled. "I've written a book on the sexual practices of the Uganda tribesman, you know. More than seven hundred pages of manuscript. No one will ever publish it, of course. I haven't even tried. When the book is complete I'll forward it to the British Museum for use by scholars. By that time I'll be retired out of the service, anyway."

"I'd like to have a look at that book."

"I'm afraid I can't let you," Niles said. "There are parts of it I couldn't show to any friend of mine. I've—conducted some very unusual research, you see. I'd hate to have you read about it."

We let the matter drop there, and I never went into it again. I suppose Geoff was sleeping with some of the native women, or doing similar things which he felt should be done for the sake of scholarship, but which he didn't want to admit to his friends. After all, the best way to find out how an African woman makes love is to make love to her yourself—but very few anthropologists would go to that extent. Geoff evidently had. I couldn't blame him for wanting to keep his research private until after his retirement or death.

About noon the next day, we came to a small village, and Geoff said, "This is the place." He pulled up the Land Rover and we got out.

Several natives came up to us. Geoff greeted them in their own language, and a long conversation ensued. They seemed to know him well and to be on good terms with him. I stood to one side, feeling very much left out of things.

When the pow-wow was over, Geoff turned to me and said, "We couldn't have timed it better. The *ugala* is going to start in about two hours. We'll have to continue on foot from here. He says practically the whole village is at the dance-site now."

With the natives to guide us, we started out. The jungle grew increasingly thick as we walked. I felt close to the collapsing point, but Geoff strode on as though he renewed his vigor with every step, and I grimly forced myself to keep up with him. After a while the sound of drum-beats became audible in the distance, soft and muffled, but growing steadily louder.

"They're warming up," Geoff said. "There's always plenty of drumming first."

We kept going. The foliage was so thick that it blocked the fierce heat of the Equatorial sun, for which I was grateful. But it was another half hour before we came to the site of the *ugala*.

It was a large clearing, perhaps a hundred feet on each side, in the heart of the jungle. Along one side of the clearing were the spectators—the old people of the tribe and the children, all of them squatting on felled logs. They looked like the impatient spectators in a baseball stadium, waiting for the game to begin.

At the other side of the clearing were the women who would dance, and perpendicular to them were seated the young males. All were wearing *futus* of the brightest colors. They were fidgeting tensely, like performers waiting for the curtain to go up.

On the fourth side of the clearing sat the drummers—about a dozen of them, squatting in front of their drums. Geoff murmured that the musicians were men who were disqualified from taking part in the dance by reason of disease, impotence, or physical disability.

No one paid any attention to us as we took seats in the back of the spectator section. The drumming continued, reaching a wild and orgiastic pitch. The drummers seemed oblivious to all about them; they stared down at their instruments with intense concentration.

Suddenly, without any signal that I noticed, the women rose and lined themselves up at one end of the clearing, and the men took positions at the other. There were about fifty of each sex.

The *ugala* began.

Geoff whispered, "It's starting now. Just sit still and don't get excited. There aren't a dozen living white men who have seen what you're going to see."

The dancers were moving slowly, in shuffling rhythmic patterns. Geoff remarked that the women with their hair piled high on their heads were the unmarried ones, and the married ones wore their hair dangling freely.

A gulf of perhaps twenty yards separated the male dancers from the female. Neither group took any notice of the others. But suddenly, as the music grew more intense, the men began to pay evident attention to the women— as they danced, the men nudged each other, pointed to the row of women, laughed, called out comments on them. The women responded by rolling their eyes flirtatiously and grinning.

This phase of the *ugala* lasted for perhaps fifteen minutes, while I sat in mounting suspense. Despite myself, I felt tremendous excitement. The dancers were acting out now the various stages of flirtation, with coyness and archness predominating. But by slow stages the action became more intense.

The men went into a frenzied dance, stamping their left foot, kicking backward with the right, shouting out wildly. They stamped their way forward until they were within ten feet of the row of girls. Then the women, giggling wildly, seized the hems of their *futus* and pulled the garments up over their faces, displaying their nude bodies completely.

Niles had told me in advance that this was a gesture of modesty, not of brazenness. It seems that exposing the face is considered wicked, while exposing the body hardly matters. By using their *futus* to cover their faces, the girls were playing shy. But they stood there, moving rhythmically, their coppery breasts and bellies and loins exposed to view, their faces hidden. As if to emphasize their strange "shyness" they turned, moving with the drilled precision of chorines, and presented their backs to the capering men—thus hiding their faces completely, and so the ultimate in Uganda modesty!

As though discouraged by this show of modesty, the men dropped back, dancing across the clearing to the far end. Now it was the turn of the girls to advance, hesitantly. The men danced in place, pretending to ignore the women, who came capering forward, extending arms and legs seductively, sometimes pulling the *futus* upward to display their loins.

Then the girls coquettishly retreated again. Advance, retreat, advance, retreat—the age-old pattern of human seduction. I felt my sweat-sticky clothes gluing themselves to my body. The dance had gone on over an hour, now; the dancers were glossy with sweat, and surely must have been close to the point of exhaustion. But still they pranced and leaped and pirouetted.

Advance, retreat, advance, retreat—until the men, pretending to be bored and disgusted by the teasing ways of the women, simply marched off into the forest. It was the cue for the girls to turn on all the juice. They went into a wild, abandoned dance now that they had the whole of the clearing to themselves. Raising their Jut us to give glimpses of their bodies, they climaxed this part of the dance by throwing off their clothing completely, hurling the garments to the edge of the clearing.

Now, I've been in nightclubs and have seen plenty of nakedness. But this was different. This wasn't any mere show-business act. This was the prelude to an orgy, and my throat was dry with anticipation. No Minsky girls these—they were going to provide the real thing for the audience, not a G-stringed fraud.

Nude, they linked arms and danced in circles. Their bodies were magnificent, muscular and brawny but still seductively feminine. Full firm breasts bobbed with each leap of the dance. Powerful buttocks gave promise of incredible sensuous pleasures. Up and down, back and forth—and now the men returned from their

hiding-place in the jungle, and the *ugala* entered its final phase at last.

They danced all together for a few minutes, and then broke up into couples, with much laughter and gaiety. While the men continued to dance, the women came up to them and unknotted their *futus*. The men's *futus* were thrown on the ground—and, as the drums beat out a colossal paradiddle of energy, the couples dropped to the ground and the desires built up during the long dance were sated.

It was startling to see the young children, five and six and even younger, watching this uninhibited display. As for me, I found the sight of fifty couples engaged in unashamed love-making tremendously overpowering. The men were of unusual stamina, the women lusty and vehement. Brown bodies writhed in sensuous delight. The drummers continued to beat.

After a while I realized that it was ending, that only a few couples remained on the mats, that the others were watching from the sidelines. I felt dazed by what I had witnessed.

Geoff murmured, "It's turning into an endurance contest now. The couple that lasts longest is supposed to be assured of long life."

I looked at him. He was still trying to maintain his anthropological detachment—but his lean face was flushed and sweaty, and I knew this had been as overpowering an experience for him as it had been for me.

We remained there until the last drumbeat had ended. Then, quietly slipping back through the woods, we set out on the journey back to Entebbe.

"Remember," Geoff warned. "Don't say a word about this to anyone in town. It could cost me my job."

I kept my word. But that first night in Entebbe I picked up a busty blonde airline stewardess and we had ourselves a ball. Never in my life did I have so much of a charge of energy to get rid of. Now that I'm back in the States, I wish I had taken just one snapshot of that incredible scene. Well, I have no photos only the vivid memory that will stay with me as long as I live. And, brother, if you get any kick from watching a barebosomed burlesque line doing bumps and grinds, take it from me—you ain't seen nothing yet!

The end

The zipper is the undoing of the modern girl, and yet, on the other hand, it opens up great possibilities.

"Sorry Miss,—I haven't seen your G-string!"

A DRINKING MAN'S
GUIDE TO EUROPE

Here's the inside story on how to have enough money on your European drinking spree to bring back a delicious assortment of liquid cheer at a fantastically low price.

by
Mal Ford

YOU'VE MANAGED somehow to scrape up the wherewithal, and you're off to Europe for a few exotic adventures of your own. One of the things that most concerns you is getting the most for your dollar when it comes to matters intoxicating. You want to know which countries offer the biggest bargains, and you want some hints on what you can bring back to this country for savoring after your return.

If you're the fellow we've described above, stick around for the next few pages. We have some useful information for you.

The first important item to remember is that you're allowed to bring back only one gallon of liquor duty-free. Anything above this is subject to Customs Duties. Since most liquor comes packaged in fifths, this means you'll be able to bring five full-sized bottles back from abroad. If you don't like that regulation, don't complain to us—write to your congressman. But

you won't get anywhere, believe me.

Don't try to smuggle more than your lawful quota into the country. You'll probably get caught, and, if you do, you'll not only have the liquor confiscated, more likely than not, but you'll get slapped with a stiff penalty too. It's smarter to declare any excess and pay the duties; if you've bought wisely abroad, you'll still be coming out ahead relative to American retail liquor prices. Another dodge which will work in limited doses is to *open* a few of the bottles and take a sip or two. You can get by Customs with two or three open bottles, since duty is only charged on sealed ones—but don't show up at the dock with fifty or a hundred uncorked flasks and expect to get away with it!

When travelling with others, find out whether anybody in the group isn't using his or her full quota. Generally you can find some teetotaler who'll be willing to import a few bottles and turn

(Continued on next page)

117

them over to you back in the States.

Now that you're set on the Customs regulations, let's have a look around the Continent and find out where the bargains are to be had.

ENGLAND is not one of them. The British share our own Puritan belief that it's perfectly proper to tax alcoholic beverages within an inch of their lives; and so, keep out of the British liquor stores. Their prices are even higher than ours, even on the famous English gins and on scotch whiskeys. If you covet Beefeater or Old Parr, you should have gone to the British West Indies, where a six-buck bottle of gin will cost you no more than $1.80 or so. However, while in England be sure to stop into the pubs and sample the local beers. Contrary to legend, they *aren't* served warm, just at room temperature. There's a dizzying variety of them in all strengths, and if you get some knowledgeable local to guide you it can be a most rewarding evening. Be sure to sample the brown ale and bitters, two varieties you won't find here. Whatever you do, don't try to buy a dry martini anywhere in the British Isles; if you get anything at all, it'll probably be a tepid half-and-half mixture of gin and vermouth.

FRANCE has some pretty steep liquor taxes too, but you can do pretty well all the same if you stick to buying bottles of the local product. Paris is loaded with liquor stores that specialize in handling the tourist trade; my favorite is Fauchon's, 26 Place de la Madeleine, which posts price-lists visibly, has a staff that speaks English, carries an enormous stock, and for a reasonable amount extra will ship your order straight back to the States or to your ship or boat.

As we said, there's nothing to be saved in France if you want gin or whiskey. But you can have a fifth of Remy Martin VSOP cognac there for $4.50, half the New York price. Delectable green chartreuse, 110 proof, is available for around $4 ($9 here.) Mumm's 1952 brut champagne will be about the same. A fifth of Benedictine is $2.50. Two bucks will get you a bottle of genuine Russian vodka—and that's just a fraction of what it would cost you in Moscow.

As you would expect, wines are cheap in France. It isn't advisable to use up your liquor quota bringing wine back, unless your taste runs to *very* expensive wine, such as Chateau Lafite-Rothschild Bordeaux, which will set you back $10 for a good vintage in New York, and less than half that in France. You can have some very fine wines with your meals for next to nothing, there—fifty francs, which is a dime, entitles you to a half-bottle of delectable *vin ordinaire* at any bistro, and for slightly more you can get superb vintage stuff. Remember, though, that plenty of clip-joints for the unwary exist in Paris.

So stock up on cognac and liqueurs

in France, if your taste runs that way. But the real bargain-country for buying liquor is SPAIN.

Spain is a tippler's paradise. For ninety cents or a dollar you can get first-rate brandy, such as Fundador or Veterano—and Fundador is five bucks in New York! Red and white table wines should run you in the vicinity of 15¢ a quart. Champagne—not the French kind, but a passable local imitation—starts at 55 a bottle. By the shot, liquor's just as cheap—2¢ for a shot of brandy, 13¢ for a reasonably decent martini.

And, of course, sherry—which is almost synonymous with Spain. There are four main kinds of sherry: the *fino*, or very dry; *amontillado*, nutty, full, not so dry; *oloroso*, the cream sherry so popular here, and *raya*, the sweetest of all. There are infinite subvarieties of these. The prices are ridiculously low—a lot less than a buck a bottle, for the same brands that sell in the $4–$6

"Her husband can't even keep her in clothes!"

range here. If you're a sherry man, don't pass up these bargains.

While you're in Spain, take a side-trip across the Straits of Gibraltar to TANGIER. Liquor prices aren't notably cheaper there than in Spain, but Tangier is the one place in the world where you can legally buy absinthe. The U.S. banned it in 1912. Absinthe is a 136-proof joy-juice made on a wormwood base, and if you drink it long enough it's guaranteed to soften up your brain. However, one shot won't do any harm, or even a whole bottle if judiciously stretched. The cost is about a buck and a half. Whatever you do, confine your absinthe-tasting experiments to Tangier. If you try to bring a bottle back to the States and get caught, you'll find yourself in very very hot water indeed!

Having been to Spain, you've skimmed off the best bargains, thanks to Spain's deflated economy. Another country where the drinkables can be had cheaply is neutral AUSTRIA. The wines and beers of Austria are glorious, as well as gloriously cheap; the Austrian champagne isn't bad either, and it's less expensive than the French variety.

For a couple of bucks a bottle you can pick up good local *schnapps*, of wide varieties. Also investigate *slivovitz*, the fiery plum brandy.

If you get up to SCANDINAVIA, different bargains await you. Denmark, of course, is the home of Cherry Heering—and this silky liqueur, which retails for seven or eight bucks a bottle in the United States, can be had for prices that will make your jaw drop, in Denmark. In any Scandinavian country you can do well with *akvavit*, a potato-mash drink not too well known in this country, and, of course, Scandinavian beer is famed justly all over the world.

Back to the bargain counter again in YUGOSLAVIA. Relatively few Americans trek to Titoland, but those who do find the journey worthwhile, liquorwise. You can begin with a powerful dark beer called *pivo*, at the munificent sum of seven cents a pint. For twice that sum, you can have a quart of wine, with the country's best wines running to the overwhelmingly high figure of 50¢ a quart.

For a half-buck, too, you can—and should—buy a bottle of *kirsch*, a colorless, vodka-like liquor brewed from cherries. A real kick to this one, and you can't go wrong at that price! Also a local favorite is a cherry brandy, not very expensive and nice as an after-dinner liqueur. The national drink, though, is *sljivovica*, our old friend *slivovitz*. This stuff is so cheap it's ridiculous, and as the Yugoslavs brew it is *potent*, and how! You can store a fifth of it in your suitcase for about the price of a shoeshine.

Even more exotic is a trip to FINLAND, and there are plenty of exotic drinks up there to sample. Two liqueurs are worth notice: *lakka* and *mesimarja*, brewed from various Arctic berries. The adventurous will like to try *paloviina*, which will curl the eyebrows of the weak, or else *jaloviina*, which is about as smooth startling drinking experiences with these little-known Finnish drinks, but you'd better have a sturdy stomach!

You don't want to miss GREECE, either. The Greek drinking specialties are *metaxa*, *ouzo*, and *raki*, and the prices are l-o-w. Also some good wines to be had.

Wines are the chief attraction in GERMANY. Beer too, of course. There isn't much here to attract you price-wise if you intend to bring stuff back home with you, but make sure to sample the dark beers and the light wines particularly.

As for ITALY, that tourist favorite, prices are a bit on the high side except for the local wines, which are good and startlingly cheap. Avoid Italian beer. The Italian gins and brandies are on the so-so side. But hunt up a velvety liqueur called *Galliano*. It's about ten bucks a bottle in this country, a lot less in its homeland, and it's just about the most tongue-caressing stuff ever to be bottled. Incidentally, be careful when you try to order a Martini in Italy. The Italian waiters usually think you mean a glass of Martini & Rossi vermouth and that's what you get—straight vermouth.

And, to cover the rest of tourist Europe briefly:

BELGIUM—excellent beer; prices expensive, to say the least.

SCOTLAND—Don't plan on picking up Scotch for a song here. The taxes are staggering, and it's no cheaper than it is in New York. The local beers are first-rate, though.

IRELAND—Prices are good in Eire, even better if you do your buying in the free port of Shannon. Make sure to salt away a bottle of Irish whiskey, and investigate Eire's one liqueur, Irish Mist. In western Ireland, make it a point to sample poteen, the local potato whiskey.

LUXEMBOURG—liquor and food are cheap here, cigarettes expensive. They tell me that absinthe is also legal here, but it isn't as easy to find as it is in Tangier.

PORTUGAL—Port wine, of course. Also all kinds of Portuguese liqueurs and brandies, not very expensive.

MONACO—Prices about the same

as France, except in the clip-joints. Be warned.

SWITZERLAND—Prices are reasonable. There are three locally-brewed liquors worth a taste: marc, kirsch, and pflumli.

As for the Iron Curtain countries, few bargains are to be had. Prices are high, high, and higher. Quality is low. POLAND brews something sold in most European countries as Polish White Spirits—140 proof, colorless, and as mild as a pint of concentrated sulphuric. Russian vodka costs a fortune in RUSSIA, less in France. CZECHOSLOVAKIA has some excellent beers. That's about the size of it.

You can see from this survey that a shrewd dispenser of moolah can pile up quite some sizable bargains, both in his on-the-spot drinking and in making use of his one-gallon import privilege. The big factor in the high cost of liquor in this country is the Government—what with Federal tax, and import duties, a bottle of Spanish brandy that starts out at 85¢ ends up at $5.50, with half a dozen middlemen extracting their profits along the way. You can do a lot better for yourself on the spot, most anywhere in Europe except for the high-liquor-tax countries like England.

American liquor taxes don't prevail on shipboard, either, so if you're taking a boat across the Atlantic you can do right nicely. For instance, if you take a Dutch freighter across you can guzzle Heineken's Beer at a dime a throw, or buy Holland Gin at a dollar a bottle—and also take your pick of wines, liquors, and cognacs of plenty of other nations. On a French Line ship, the champagne flows freely and cheaply. The trouble is that on the return voyage everyone stocks up, and if you don't move fast you're liable to find yourself left out. It's best to set aside your import quota before boarding the ship, just to take no chances.

It's also a clever idea to drop into your local liquor store and ascertain prices before starting out. Liquor

prices vary all over the country; generally, imported stuff is cheaper in the east than in the west, because of the additional cost of shipping across the country. State taxes also add variables to the equation. But if you're not familiar with the prices, you may be doing yourself out of the biggest buys. Take France, for instance. A fifth of fine champagne and a fifth of fine cognac have about the same price. Yet the champagne sells for $7 here and the cognac for $9, so you're a lot better off having brought back the brandy instead of the bubbly.

There's just one big trouble with buying your liquor abroad at bargain-basement prices. You bring back a fine bottle of *oloroso* sherry from Spain. Price, 65¢. You drink it. Sooner or later, sadly, it's gone. You liked it. You liked it a whole lot. So you hie yourself down to the local liquor store and ask the man for a bottle of the same. He takes it down, bristling with tax stamps.

The price is $6.33.

Plus sales tax.

You hie yourself back home, either sore of heart or else sore of pocket-book.

It's insidious. You cultivate tastes that way which you can't afford to maintain. Or, what's worse, you find yourself hipped in Finnish paloviina or something else equally impossible to obtain here. And you stare mournfully and long at the empty bottle, wishing you had some more.

There's a simple solution, pal. Save your pennies, get on the boat, get going back to Europe for another swing through the liquor stores of the Continent. Replenish your stock. The second time around, you'll be a real expert; you won't make any of the mistakes you did on your first trip. You'll have one hell of a fine time—and when you get back home, the cupboard will once again be stocked with goodies. So—bon voyage on your next exotic adventure!

The End

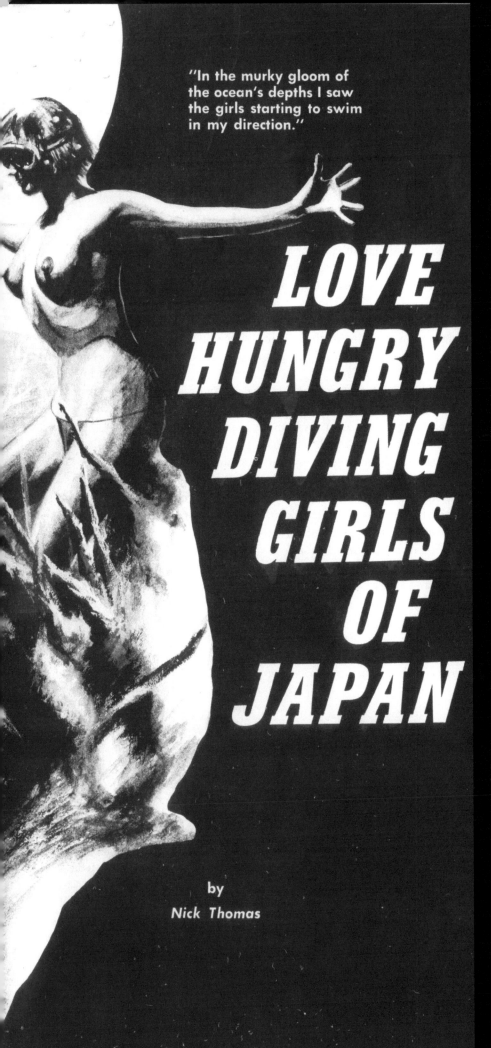

"In the murky gloom of the ocean's depths I saw the girls starting to swim in my direction."

LOVE HUNGRY DIVING GIRLS OF JAPAN

by

Nick Thomas

IT WAS ONE HELL of a shock to be surrounded by naked girls fifty feet below the surface of the Pacific Ocean. I was busy stuffing oysters into a burlap bag when the attackers came. There were half a dozen of them, slim and graceful, wearing nothing but a strand of cloth around their loins. Astonished, I looked up from the oyster bed, saw them with their long black hair floating out behind them, their bare breasts swimming toward me like pale fish.

I was skin-diving for pearls off the coast of Honshu. My partner, Cal Rush, was supposedly waiting up there on the surface for me to finish my half-hour stint. We had set up shop on this little uninhabited speck of land just off-shore. We were figuring to make a fortune skindiving in the pearl beds. With an investment of no more than a couple hundred bucks for skindiving equipment and a boat, we planned on making a return of five or six thousand dollars each—enough to set us up in Japan in regal style.

Only we didn't stop to think that we might be poaching on somebody else's preserve. Until, all of a sudden, the water was thick with naked girls.

They swarmed all around me, seemingly untroubled by the depth and the pressure and the extreme cold. The fact that I had a scuba outfit and they were naked didn't seem to trouble them either. They crawled all over me, pinioning my arms and legs, and one of them reached out and yanked my mouthpiece out. I got panicky. Now I was on an even footing with them—except they were trained for underwater endurance, and I wasn't.

I was flopping around down there like a drawing fish. Slowly we started

(Continued on next page)

123

to rise to the surface, with a naked girl hanging on to each of my limbs, and two others directing the proceedings. I was gulping water and too sick to resist. We came to the top; I gasped, wanted to throw up. All around me, female heads were bobbing. I saw our little rowboat, with Cal sitting in it looking shamefaced and bewildered. Three girls were sitting in the boat with him, and five more were in a big flat-bottomed boat of their own hauled up alongside. The girls were all in their early twenties, maybe even younger, and not one of them was wearing a stitch save for the abbreviated loincloth that was nothing more than a strand of rope twisted around the hips.

They dumped me unceremoniously into my boat. I sat there, retching and gasping. When I could speak, I said to Cal, "What the hell is this?"

"We were on their territory," he said. "They grabbed me before I knew what was happening, and sent down some girls to get you. They're the *ama*. The professional lady pearl divers."

I nodded dully. One of the naked girls had taken our oars and was rowing us toward shore. Her body was lean and muscular; she was facing me as she rowed, and I saw the muscles rippling behind her small, tip-tilted breasts. She seemed quite unconcerned about her nudity. Looking back, I saw the girls in the other boat lowering themselves over its side, throwing cork tubs over the side and diving down head-first. Some of them were down for nearly two minutes, and when they came up they had fistfuls of oysters. These they dumped into the tubs on the surface, and then they went below for more. It

was fantastic. Cal and I had gone about gathering the oysters in the modern way—taking turns with the scuba rig, going down for half an hour at a time and frog-flipping around until we had all the oysters we could handle. But these girls went down naked, equipped only with goggles, and yet their powers of breath and endurance seemed practically superhuman.

We reached the shore. In Japanese our rower said curtly, *"Out."* We got out.

The beach was deserted except for us and this strange little band of naked girls. The others were coming ashore now, having finished their diving for the day. Cal and I glanced uneasily around.

"What now?" I asked.

"We might as well apologize for poaching on their territory and get out of here," he said. He started back toward the boat to get our gear together. But a couple of the girls hopped lithely over to cut him off. We noticed now that they had taken knives from their boat, and had thrust them in their loincloths. The knives looked ugly, and the girls looked like they wouldn't think twice about using them.

"We want to leave," Cal said awkwardly, in lame Japanese. "We meant no harm. We didn't realize the oyster bed was being worked by others."

"You will stay here."

Prodding us with the scabbards of their knives, they kept us away from the boats. The girls were bronzed evenly all over, as though long exposure to the sun of their naked bodies was customary. Their bodies were lean, and without exception their breasts were small but finely formed. Japanese women do not have bulky breasts, but what they have is almost invariably shapely.

They led us up-beach to a good-sized hut and showed us inside. Inside, they milled around, examining us critically. It was unnerving to be cooped up like this with a dozen or

fifteen bare-bosomed wenches. One of the girls seemed to be the leader—a tall one, as Japanese girls go, with firm, high, pointed breasts and silken skin that glowed with a lovely sheen. Her name was Nakki, she told us—and she gave us some long-awaited explanations.

The girls were indeed *ama*, female pearl divers. This was their special territory that Cal and I had moved in on, and they couldn't stand for that. It was one of the richest oyster beds in the area that we had landed on through sheer blind luck.

We learned that the girls got a ridiculous thirty yen a day—less than two dollars American money—and, for this, they worked eight hours a day. The reason the pearl bed was so rich was because these were cultured pearls. The girls were employed by the great Nichimura cultured-pearl combine. They dove down, brought up oysters in which grains of sand would be inserted, and replaced elsewhere those that had already been seeded. The oysters would secrete pearls around the irritating grains of sand placed within themselves. Hence, nearly every oyster in a seeded area would contain a cultured pearl. And these would fetch good prices, though naturally not anywhere near what natural pearls commanded.

"All right," I said, when Nakki had finished telling us this. "We had no idea this was anyone's private cache of cultured pearls. We'll be glad to leave right away and we hope you'll forgive us for blundering in here like this."

She shook her head. "No. You may not leave."

"Not leave?"

"You will have to remain here until the harvest is complete. It will be another month. Otherwise you might betray us."

Cal and I swore up and down that we wouldn't do any such thing, but it was no good. It seems that the cultured pearl business is a fantastically competitive racket in Japan. If we were to leave with the knowledge of where the Nichimura cultured-pearl bed was located, we would—the girls feared—sell our knowledge to one of the other big combines. And then one of Nichimura's competitors might send boats here to destroy the oyster beds or even to steal the seeded oysters. No—under no condition could we leave here until the harvest was complete. And that meant cooling our heels here for a month, not to be released until it was too late for us to do any betraying.

We were left alone in the hut, placed under guard. I felt cold and miserable, since I was still in my skindiving outfit. At least Cal was dry.

He shrugged. "You think we ought to try to make a break for it? Those girls look like they mean business with their stickers."

"It would be risky. They take this job damned seriously."

"But we can't hang around here on this godforsaken island a whole month."

I smiled. "We've got fifteen pretty girls to look at. We won't be completely bored."

Before the week was out, I had reason to eat those words—with soy sauce.

We paced up and down inside the hut until it grew dark. The girls were on the water constantly, working in shifts. We talked to our guard and learned that they had been here for two weeks already, with nearly four weeks of work left before they could return to the mainland. And we were the first men they had seen in those two weeks!

I should have been terrified when I heard that. Instead I rejoiced—like the fool that I was.

The lovemaking started that night, after dinner. The girls fed us on raw fish, seaweed, and saki—not a very appetizing meal, you might say, but we were so hungry we'd have eaten everything. And then, giggling, they swarmed all over Cal and me.

If you've never been swarmed over by fifteen naked wenches, you've missed an experience, believe me. We were at the bottom of a heap of warm, soft arms and legs and thighs and breasts and bellies and buttocks, and to the accompaniment of shrill girlish laughter they pulled off our clothes and, in the semi-darkness, fought with each other for the right to make love with us.

I began to realize that the girls were delighted to hold us prisoners. It was not so much loyalty to their employer as it was downright sex starvation that gave them the idea of keeping us around. None of them were married, and their work was hellishly difficult and dangerous. The only enjoyment in their life was sex, and usually they couldn't get any of that until their seeding stint was up and they returned to the mainland. But now they had us…

And did they ever have us! That first night it must have been half a dozen times for each of us, until we were dizzy and reduced to a dull stupor. And still they came, crawling over us, putting our hands on their little warm breasts, flattening their bodies against ours, grunting with delight…

At last they let us sleep. We sprawled out on the floor of the hut. The next thing I knew, it was day; the sun was streaming in. The hut was empty, all but Cal, who lay like a dead man over at the far side. One off-duty girl stood outside the hut, a knife unsheathed in her hand. They

**Of course I love you.
It's just that our hour is up.**

weren't going to let us escape, that was for sure.

I looked past her, out to the sea, and there I saw the boat anchored, and the girls coming up and going over the side. I went back into the hut and lay down again on the floor.

Cal awoke. "How do you feel?" he asked.

"Like I've been through a concrete mixer."

"Same here. Those girls really give you a workout."

"Another night like that will kill me," I groaned.

I was wrong, of course. It didn't kill me, merely brought me to the edge of breakdown. The girls weren't so violent this night. They waited their turns politely. But their appetites were insatiable. I began to know what it's like to be put out to stud. Fun at first, but then sheer brutal hard work.

It became a routine. The girls would dive all day, make love all night. Cal and I were outnumbered, and we couldn't fight them off. We spent all day recuperating and sleeping. They fed us plenty of oysters, and maybe the old legends about the aphrodisiac powers of oysters are true, because some of my feats those few days went beyond what I thought my own capacity was.

By the fifth night, though, Cal and I were both pretty desperate. We had lost a lot of weight and we were so groggy we could hardly walk straight.

It was midday, the sixth day. The girls were far out on the water, all except the guard.

I said hoarsely to Cal, "We can't

keep this up for a whole month. We'll turn into gibbering lunatics. Into nervous wrecks."

"It's a scream," he said hollowly. "Fifteen passionate lovely young girls, and we're plotting ways to escape from them!"

"I know. But we've got to get out of here."

"How?"

"We'll have to take our chances with that knife. If we can get past the girl on duty, we can make a break for our boat down on shore. Then we just row like hell for the mainland."

"How are you going to get that knife away from the girl out there?"

"Leave it to me," I said.

I crawled to the doorway and called to her. "Meiki! Meiki!"

She turned and peered in. "What do you want?"

"The other American is asleep," I whispered. "Come here and we will make love."

"Now?"

"Yes, now. Before the other girls return. I will show you things you never dreamed of."

She looked tempted. After all, these girls weren't very bright. Cal was pretending to snore, and I was trying to look sincere. After a couple of moments of inward debate, the girl tiptoed into the hut.

"We must be quick," she whispered.

She was about seventeen, and the saltwater hadn't yet had much of an effect on her skin. She melted into my arms, and I caressed her soft curved buttocks, her gentle rounded breasts, her warm pale thighs. She had parked the knife on the floor, out of my reach. As we lay together, body to body, I signaled Cal. He rose, picked up a cooking pot, tiptoed toward us. The girl in my arms was gasping in passion. She never noticed him. Not until the pot bounced ringingly off her skull and she went limp in my arms.

I put her gently down. "I hope you didn't kill her," I said.

"She's just got a nasty bump, that's all. Come on, you idiot!" Cal hissed.

"Don't moon over her now!"

We grabbed up the knife, just in case, and raced down the beach to the place where our boat was drylanded. We pushed it down to the waves and got in. All our gear was still stowed safely away.

The girls were well out from shore now, more than a hundred and fifty yards. We saw their glistening bronze bodies, sleek and shiny as those of seals, flashing in the sunlight. They saw us, too. They let out outraged screams and started pulling up anchor.

"Row!" Cal yelled. "Pull! Pull!"

I pulled as if my life depended on it—which it did. Another three weeks of captivity would have finished me. I rowed until I was exhausted, and then Cal took over. The girls were giving pursuit, but we had a five-minute head start on them, and their boat was bigger, heavier, and slower.

We rounded the island and, reaching inland waters, streaked for shore. It was a mile-wide strait, and just try rowing a mile in choppy water when you're just at the threshold of exhaustion. We looked back, though, and saw that the girls had given up.

Half an hour later we were ashore. We stowed our gear away at the pier and staggered to our hotel a few blocks away. We collapsed on our beds and slept right around the clock.

Funny—I had strange dreams. Dreams of fifteen slim naked girls swarming over me, making love.

It was a month before I felt the need of a woman again. I had had enough sex in that single week to last me quite a while, let me tell you. Cal felt the same way. There have been times since when I've had to go long spells without having a woman, but I console myself by remembering the one time when more sex was available than I could possibly handle.

We abandoned our skindiving project and got other jobs. And, to this day, I break out in a cold sweat whenever I see a woman wearing a necklace of cultured pearls.

The end

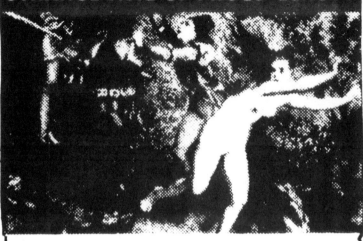

JUAREZ

SIN CITY ACROSS THE BORDER

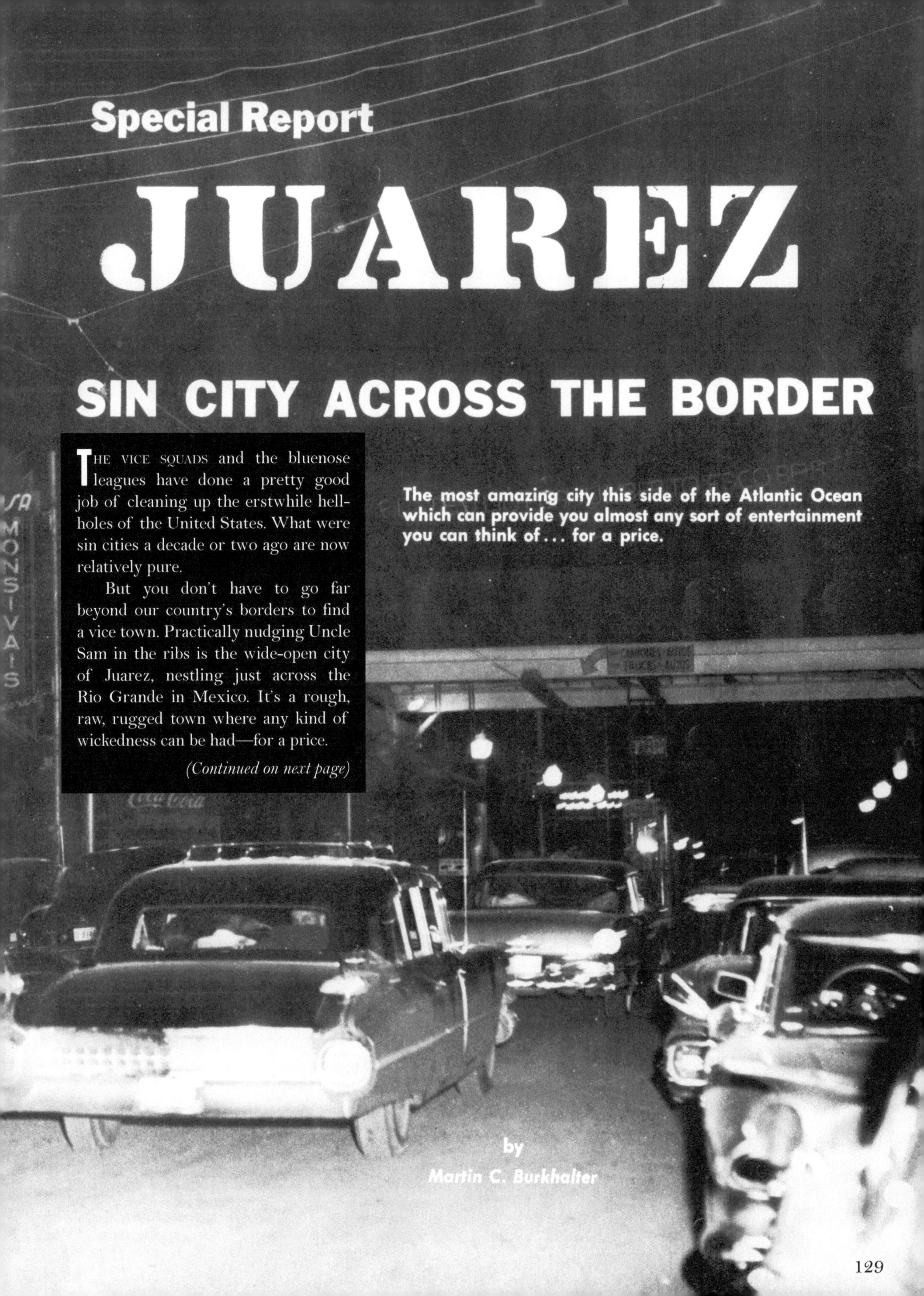

THE VICE SQUADS and the bluenose leagues have done a pretty good job of cleaning up the erstwhile hell-holes of the United States. What were sin cities a decade or two ago are now relatively pure.

But you don't have to go far beyond our country's borders to find a vice town. Practically nudging Uncle Sam in the ribs is the wide-open city of Juarez, nestling just across the Rio Grande in Mexico. It's a rough, raw, rugged town where any kind of wickedness can be had—for a price.

(Continued on next page)

The most amazing city this side of the Atlantic Ocean which can provide you almost any sort of entertainment you can think of... for a price.

by
Martin C. Burkhalter

No passport is needed to get there. You start out from El Paso, Texas, stroll across the International Bridge, and you're in Juarez, North America's capital of lewdness. It's a total journey of some ten minutes from the land of the free and the home of the brave.

Juarez is an all-night town. The main drag sparkles with garish neon as a come-on for the droves of fun-happy Americans who come dollar-laden across the bridge every night. Not so brightly lit are the narrow, winding side streets where modern-day Mexican bandits lie in waiting to relieve unwary tourists of their belongings. And wherever you look, your eye will come to rest on bars and bordellos by the score. Bold and brassy Juarez knows where the money lies. Last year better than two million tourists poured a cool $55,000,000 into Juarez, and they're figuring to do even better this year.

As a special investigator for *Exotic Adventures*, we crossed the border to have a look-see at this fabulous town. It's quite a place—though not for your Aunt Nellie. Sex and souvenirs are the big industries. And the prices are gaspers.

A bourbon-and-water runs 90¢ to $1.25 almost anywhere. Beer is half a buck to 75¢ for a *glass*. Little cheap gewgaws in the souvenir shops bear sizzling price-tags. And the tourists buy them. There must be something about the atmosphere in Juarez that persuades the American suckers to toss their cash away so lightheartedly.

You walk down the main strip, the Avenida Juarez. Here's the Folies Burlesque, with photos of bare-breasted cuties pasted all around the front as a come-on. You go inside, separating yourself from a couple of bucks in the process. You see dim lights, a small stage, an eager audience crammed as close as they can get. A tenth-rate band is playing, and a girl is taking off her clothes. There isn't anything very subtle about it. The girl is about eighteen, Mexican. She's chunky, with thick ankles—but who looks at her ankles? She whips off her clothes in rhythm to the oom-pah coming from the band, and gives you a look at young, full breasts with their nipples concealed by spangles. She dances around quickly and gets off stage, wiggling her provocative buttocks at you before she vanishes.

She's followed by another girl, somewhat older, a lot more slinky. This one takes more time to get out of her clothes, and there are no spangles on the nipples this time. Clad only in G-string, she gives herself a vigorous body shake, and you watch her more-than-ample mounds of flesh quiver erotically. A few of the customers in the front row reach out for the G-string, but she laughs and jumps back.

The band plays for a while, and then the main attraction comes out. She's tall—a six-footer, perhaps—and she's in no rush at all to take it off. She sings, badly, and peels slowly, undulating seductively, gliding between the tables, occasionally giving a goggle-eyed customer a sisterly kiss on the cheek. They drool and snatch at her, but she's too quick for them. The music gets more frenzied; the girl gets rid of everything but bra and panties, and then the bra goes. High, jutting breasts, glistening with oil, shine in the spotlights. Then the panties go. There's not even a G-string on this girl. For one frozen moment she stands on stage absolutely naked; then there's a blackout and when the lights go up, she's gone.

Afterward, the strippers return, skimpily but adequately covered, and circulate among the patrons, cadging drinks. The visitors jostle each other out of the way to have the privilege of forking over a buck and a quarter to buy their favorite a drink—and, of course, the drink is just tea, or else colored water.

The no-G-string business is a Juarez highlight, and it isn't always featured. It goes in waves. One month the style is total nudity; then there come complaints from the armed forces camps across the borders, and the Mex authorities clamp down and insist on G-strings. After a few weeks, they're back to total display.

You leave the Folies Burlesque and wander on. Plenty of other clubs offer nudery—the Latin Quarter, Club Fausto, the Guadalajara, and plenty more. The Club Fausto was offering when I was there, a specialty stripper named Cassandra, who had specially trained pectoral muscles. The pectoral muscles are the ones that control the motions of the breasts, and Cassandra did some unbelievable things with her robust mammaries. Also at the Fausto was a well-stacked stripped called Cristina who has a large following of enthusiastic fans, and who was just about the prettiest girl we saw in Juarez.

At the Latin Quartre, a statuesque blonde performed a reenactment of Lady Godiva's ride for us, and then, as an encore, did a weird dance in which a pair of fluorescent hands painted on her buttocks provided the exotic touch. And the Guadalajara, as its contribution to Juarez night life, was featuring a midget stripper, around three-feet-six but beautifully proportioned for her height.

A lot of visitors to Juarez are satisfied with a trip to the burleycue houses. Others are in search of more personal entertainment.

For them, there's a red-light district covering 8 blocks by 12 blocks. There everything is available from the cheapest, sleaziest kind of sex to elegant high-toned stuff. As you stroll through the neighborhood, men who look like caricatures of what they are come slithering up to you, offering filthy books, filthy movies, filthy shows, filthy anything.

We went straight to the office of the *Department de Accion Medico Sociale*, or Department of Health. There we saw an enormous file containing registration cards for each of Juarez' prostitutes. Close to 900 were registered with the Department.

It's the Department's job to maintain some kind of semblance of order in Juarez. It's illegal, for instance, to be a streetwalker—all Juarez girls must operate indoors. So when the local gendarmerie pick up a stroller, they turn her over to the Department to be registered and assigned to a house. She has to produce a birth certificate proving she's 18, the minimum age for Juarez chippies, and she's required to show up for a weekly medical examination. If she misses a turn, she gets shut up in a penal dormitory for a while. Prostitution is all very tightly regulated in Juarez, you see.

The girls get penicillin shots at a nominal cost to keep them free from disease. The girls are watched closely and are not permitted to cross the border. Any Juarez girl caught in El Paso gets hustled right back to Mexico pronto.

An officer of the Juarez vice squad took me on a guided tour of the red light district. There were no neon signs here. It was as squalid and as dirty as any slum neighborhood you care to name. Although it was fairly late in the evening, toddlers of two and three were still up and wandering around, naked, in the streets. The brothels were jam-packed, one next to the other. My guide picked out one at random, saying, "One's just like the next. Let's start here."

About a dozen girls sat lumped back on benches just inside the door. They ranged in age from the late teens up to about forty, and they ranged in attractiveness from pretty nice down

to utterly slovenly. The younger and prettier girls were fairly neatly dressed, with everything covered up. Some of the older women were a lot less formal. One had her blouse completely unbuttoned, revealing heavy, sagging breasts. Another wore no skirt, only a garter-belt and cotton stockings. A third had her skirt up above her knees.

We talked with some of the girls. Business wasn't so good tonight— the soldiers had been in yesterday, and today they were broke. The girls didn't mind telling us about themselves. The oldest had been in the business seventeen years. She averaged a hundred dollars a week, which is a young fortune in Mexico, and she had saved enough to allow her to retire soon.

None of the girls seemed especially bitter about their profession. The older ones actually enjoyed their work; the younger ones simply shrugged and said, "It is better than starving. We are treated well, we do not get disease, and we do not suffer."

"How much do you charge?" I asked the prettiest.

She got $3.50, she said, except when a client was so obviously wealthy that she could ask more. $25 bought her services for the whole night. Out of every $3.50, she turned over all but 85¢ to her boss. Even so, she did all right, netting $15 and $20 on a fairly good night, and up to $45 when the soldiers came over from El Paso in big numbers. Divide $45 by 85¢ and you'll see that these girls have very very busy evenings indeed.

Talking to the girls, I discovered that one of their biggest problems is dope addiction. The girls have plenty of money, by Mexican standards, and they're easily victimized by unscrupulous pushers. About half the girls admitted that they had had narcotics trouble at some time or other, and they told me that one of their colleagues was thrown out just the other day for being caught by the boss in the act of taking on a load of junk. Naturally, the Federal authorities are aware of the

Scanti-Wear Chic Parisian

132

prevalence of addiction in Juarez, and they expend plenty of effort to keep drugs from slipping across the border at this vulnerably point.

We left then, and moved on to another bawdy house, somewhat more impressive. This was one of the houses that catered to a mixed clientele of thrill-hungry tourists. When we walked in, we saw a few American couples at the bar, looking very uneasy and shamefaced. They hadn't come for sex themselves, naturally—they had come to watch.

This is a specialty of several Juarez houses. For about $5 a piece, you can view another couple. The males are usually local lusty lads who pick up some nice cash and get a little free fun in the process—but at a couple of places, there are peephole arrangements so you can watch legitimate customers making love to the girls of the house. You pay more for this kind of show.

Also a big feature is the "French Show," which is a movie screening held at many Juarez bordellos. I saw one. Other films show, anything. If you know how to ask, you can be shown it all in Ciudad Juarez.

You can buy anything, too. Filthy pictures? The peddlers flock around. Pornographic books? Just shell out the moolah and you can take your pick of the best, imported from France— Henry Miller, the Marquis de Sade, Guillaume Apollinaire, and loads of non-classic erotic literature. Also easily available are lewd comic books, "the kind men like"—the sort in which familiar comic book characters are depicted in obscene situations.

In addition, Juarez is well organized for dealing in vice!

We moved on again, going from brothel to brothel until I got tired of seeing the same repetitious stuff. In some places the girls would be nearly nude, in others fully dressed, and all of them were polite and somewhat bored. None of the prostitutes displayed themselves in total nudity, not out of modesty but simply because total

nudity tends to diminish the sex drive, while partial nudity—long stockings, a bra, panties, etc.—arouses curiosity and desire.

We finished our tour at the Rio Rosa, which is one of Juarez' most celebrated bawdy houses. There was a long bar, at which some of the prettier girls persuaded amorous tourists to unload as much cash as possible before going into one of the closet-sized bedrooms to take care of the main purpose of his visit. I saw a couple of soldiers too drunk to know what branch of the service they were in, reeling around at the bar. They corralled two girls and vanished into the bedroom section in the rear of the place. They were back in less than five minutes, looking sweaty and satisfied. A couple of minutes later the girls were back at the bar, hunting for their next customers.

And so it went, on through the night. Strip shows, B-girls, prostitutes, pimps, hawkers of filth of all kinds— they did boom business well along toward dawn. As the sun came up, a strange and eerie calm settled over Juarez. It's the same calm that comes over Las Vegas or any other town totally dedicated to night life. Juarez slept. It would not begin to come back to life again until noon—and then it would roar full blast far into the next morning.

Quite a place. Now that Fidel Castro has cleaned up Havana to a large measure, Juarez is practically unique. It's a town where anything goes, where prostitution is legal and regulated by the authorities, where the police are only on hand to make sure that nobody gets murdered or robbed.

Otherwise, everything is permitted. It's a town without blue laws, and it can come as a stunning shock to any innocent American raised in a state where gambling is prohibited, where eager-beaver do-gooders see to it that sexual scenes are deleted from the movies, where the bars have to close at certain hours. The people of Juarez think that our blue laws are just fine. They wish the United States was

even more strait-laced than it is now.

Because the tighter the anti-sex laws are drawn in gringoland, the greater the numbers of Americans who will flock across the International Bridge to seek forbidden pleasures in Ciudad Juarez. Juarez has only one commodity to sell, and it's a commodity people want. So long as there are laws interfering with the rights of Americans to seek whatever pleasures they want, Juarez will remain, a festering hellhole of depravity, a wide-open town just across the border from Texas.

The end

I ESCAPED FROM THE SOVIET SLAVE CAMP

OCTOBER, 1956, Budapest—revolution! We hoped it would be the beginning of a new era for our suffering Hungary. Instead it has meant, for my country, redoubled anguish under the brutal Soviet heel. And, for me, it meant two years of hideous defilement in a Soviet slave camp beyond the borders of Siberia.

I was twenty-three in the fateful October. That meant I was old enough to remember the terrors of the war years, but that most of my life had been spent in a Hungary ruthlessly

(Continued on next page)

by
Anna Lukacs
As told to Les Fields

compelled to serve the Red master. Like many young Hungarians I quietly resented the presence of the Russian soldiers in our cities. I despised the Stalinist puppets who ruled us, taking orders from the Kremlin.

All during 1955 and 1956, we had been whispering to ourselves. I need not repeat here the story of the Hungarian Revolution, except to say that my husband, Erno Lucaks, who was killed in the revolution, was among the leaders. Erno and I were both students at Budapest University, where many of the revolutionaries attended. We had been married in the spring of 1956, and we lived in a pitiful little dingy flat in Budapest. Six months of married life was all that was to be allotted to us.

October 23, 1956—the first open rioting, in the gardens of the National Museum, after a summer of ominous rumbling. Erno and I were there. With hundreds of other young Hungarians, we demanded the return of full national independence, the end of the Red puppet regime. You know how our cry spread throughout Hungary, how within five days we had almost completely liberated our country before the stunned dictators reacted.

By October 31, the brave general Pal Maleter, martyred by Khrushchev's gangsters later, was in control of Budapest and the western half of the country. In the east, Soviet troops were hard put to defend themselves. The next day, Imre Nagy—also a martyr—declared Hungry a neutral country.

You all know the grim events that followed—how on November 4, just as we began to believe we had actually defeated the Soviet colossus, the Red tanks ground into Hungary, bringing death in their wake. Thousands died in the next week; more than a hundred thousand, realizing defeat was inevita-

ble, fled across the border into Austria and safety.

That was the story of the rape of Hungary in 1956. Let me now tell my own story of Soviet shame.

My husband Erno died in the fighting on November 7. I saw him struck down in the street. He died instantly. That night my friends urged me to flee across the border. "Come with us into Austria," they begged. "Hungary is doomed. There will be no help from the West, and we cannot hold off the Soviets ourselves any longer."

But I refused to leave. I told them I would continue to fight until my last drop of blood had moistened Hungarian soil. What could I gain by running to safety? I had nothing to live for, now that my husband was dead, nothing but the continued struggle for Hungarian freedom. And I could not fight that from exile.

The massacre continued for another week. But the Soviets, conscious of the terrible propaganda consequences of the brutal suppression of my country, and aware that they had been victorious already, decided to cease the murdering and to take prisoners instead. Hundreds of us were rounded up in a single twenty-four-hour period. We were all taken to a large room in one of the government buildings, and there we were interrogated.

The interrogation was short and typically Soviet. We were questioned one at a time. If a man refused to answer, he was kicked in the groin. If a woman kept silent, her breasts were slapped. Further tortures were reserved for the most stubborn.

I came before the inquisitioner and stood silent as he asked me my name and profession.

"Answer!"

I glared at him. "Butcher!" I hissed. He nodded. A subordinate ripped

open my already tattered blouse. My breasts, which only my dead husband had ever touched, were bare before their lustful eyes. A hand rose; I felt a stinging burst of pain as the thick palm slapped me. I bit my lip to keep from fainting.

After five minutes of this treatment I whispered, "Anna Lukacs—student."

All students were set aside for deportation. The Soviets reasoned that we, the Hungarian intellectuals, were the most dangerous enemies, and had to be removed from the country. Together with a few dozen of my young comrades, I huddled miserably in a locked room, trying to hold the tatters of my blouse closed over my throbbing breasts.

None of us slept that night. At three in the morning we were ordered out into the bitter cold. We marched on foot under gunpoint to the Budapest railway station. The Russian overlords had the trains all ready. We were crammed aboard one of the so-called Stolopinskies. A Stolopinsky, named after a Czarist Minister of Security, is a railroad car long used by the Russians for transporting prisoners. There were eight cages facing a narrow hallway. In each cage were three wooden shelves nine feet wide, and into each cage went fifteen prisoners, five on a shelf. We lay flat on our stomachs, wedged tightly together, our heads butting against the bars of the cages.

The horrible trip went on for weeks. We were permitted to go out twice a day to the toilet, but the rest of the time we lay on our shelves, unable to turn around, unable to lift our heads more than a foot without hitting the shelves above us. The car reeked of sweat and urine. Men and women travelled together with no regard to sex.

It was now December. We crossed bleak and barren land, passed through cities, went ever eastward. We knew where our destination lay—in Siberia, that Godforsaken land of slave camps and mines.

After weeks of agonizing travel, our trip came to a halt. The women prisoners were taken off the train and were taken to a prison camp, while the men continued their lonely journey deeper into Siberia. In a strange way, I was grateful that Erno had been killed in the fighting. It would have been more dreadful to be separated like this, living in eternal doubt. At least this way I knew he had gone to his rest.

MVD troopers welcomed us to the prison camp, for women only. We were led through the gates and taken to a huge building for indoctrination. After weeks of cramped travel, I was weak and found walking difficult, but I kept on my feet, for I noticed that whenever a woman fell she was forced back on her feet by brutal kicks and blows.

Inside the big building, we were ordered in Hungarian to remove our clothes. Braced for any sort of atrocity, I complied. It was almost a pleasure to get out of my filth-encrusted rags after so many weeks. I dumped them in a rubbish barrel and tried to ignore the hungry stares of the fifteen male guards. I reddened, and tried to cover my breasts, but my hands were thrust down to my sides by an angry MVD man.

When we were all naked, we were marched two abreast into a smaller room, where we were forced to get under an ice-cold shower. After that MVD men with shears chopped away our hair—"to prevent contamination," we were told.

Next came a brief medical examination, and—finally—the issuing of prison clothing. I was shown to my barracks. Many of the other slaves had been here since the days of World War II. They were withered, worn-out old hags. I was shocked to learn that the woman who had the lower berth of my double-decker bunk was only forty. She was a Rumanian who had been in the prison camp since 1945. She looked like a crone of sixty or seventy, with her stringy white hair and toothless mouth.

And so I entered my life as a Soviet slave. Since it was winter, there was no farming or mining possible, and instead we worked on clothing—making prison garments for other prisoners! We worked fourteen hours a day, under the supervision of MVD guards. When our work-day was over, I was happy to tumble into my bunk without a further thought.

The camp was well guarded. It was ringed by a fence twelve feet high, with machine-gun towers at regular spaces. A smaller fence was erected within the outer one. Any unauthorized person stepping over the inner fence would be shot without question.

For my first week and a half, I did nothing but work and sleep, work and sleep. My other Hungarian friends had been scattered all over the huge camp, to prevent any of us from getting together and hatching escape plans. Not that escape was a serious possibility. It was all but hopeless. Even if we could get over the barbed-wire fences, where could we go? It was a hundred miles of barren wasteland to the nearest large town, and it was thousands of miles, literally, to any free country.

I worked and slept, worked and slept. One day blurred into the next. I tried not to think about my old life, about the dead husband I had loved so much, about my mutilated country. I told myself that I would submerge myself in the backbreaking routine of work here, and pray for an early death and release from my toil.

But then a new aspect came into my life. I was tapped to minister to the lusts of my Soviet captors. Once each week we were taken to the medical area for a shower, and we were observed carefully by the women-hungry MVD guards. Most of the women were walking scarecrows. By comparison, I was a beauty, even after weeks of suffering in the railway car. My breasts still had firmness and texture, my thighs and buttocks still were fleshy and ripe. It was inevitable that I would attract the attention of one of the guards.

It happened my third shower session. I was drying off, shivering from the cold water, when a guard walked up to me and looked me over as though I were a prize farm animal he was considering purchasing. He nodded approvingly.

"Put your clothes on and come with me," he said in heavily-accented Hungarian.

Trembling nervously, I followed him out of the medical area and to a small shack near the guard dormitories. He closed the door.

"Remove your clothes."

I didn't dare refuse. I knew he could kill me on the spot if I didn't cooperate.

"Lie on the floor."

After this, I became a regular mistress for the MVD guards. I learned that there were about twenty-five of us in the camp, out of the hundreds of women. We were chosen for our looks, and the guards kept us carefully nourished, so that we would remain attractive for them while the ordinary women withered and decayed. We were slipped extra food and sometimes we were allowed to leave work early. But in return for these unwanted privileges we paid in a terrible way. Any hour of the day or night we were subject to the lusts of the Russians. One, two, a dozen of them at a time might have us.

I remember what happened when one of our group rebelled. She was a Czech girl, a member of the resistance—a handsome dark-haired girl with high, full breasts and a magnificent animal-like body full of vitality. She was one of the most popular partners the Russians had. But one day in late winter she went on strike. A guard was about to have her in the shed. She kicked him painfully and hit him.

What followed was hellish. She was dragged out, naked, and hurled onto a snowbank. There she was systematically beaten in the full view of everyone in the camp. She howled and screamed but guards held her.

When they were through, they left her. She died that night of exposure and shock.

We submitted without rebellion after that, but without pleasure either. I developed a trick of blanking out my mind. While I was compelled to submit to the caresses of my captors, I would think nothing, feel nothing, experience nothing. The Russians hated this, but though they tried every sort of treatment from gifts to punishment they were unable to make us respond ardently to them.

I might have gone on like that for years, until I was no longer attractive enough to please them, and then I would have reverted to the status of just another prisoner and would have become a haggard crone like them. But good luck—and quick thinking—saved me from this fate, and eventually gave me freedom.

It was a year after my arrival there. I had long ago lost every shred of self-respect. I was no longer a human being, merely a walking robot designed to give pleasure to my captors. And then, one day, the commandant of the camp entered the shower room while I was there.

My hair had grown in, and my body had filled out thanks to the extra food I was receiving. He was immediately taken by me. I saw him staring at my body for nearly ten minutes. Then he called one of his subordinates over and whispered.

That afternoon I was delivered to the commandant's quarters for his personal pleasure. He was in his forties, a refined-looking officer who sported a monocle.

"Undress," he said languidly.

I removed my clothes. Nude, I was forced to share vodka and caviar with him. Then we went to bed.

I might have reacted the way I did with the common soldiers. But an inspiration struck me—and, concealing my repugnance, I gave myself to him fully, imitating the passionate cries of a woman. He was surprised and pleased by this. And, the next day, I was informed that I was promoted to the rank of Commandant Kistbek's official mistress.

I pretended to be overjoyed. The Commandant had several mistresses drawn from the camp slaves, but he was displeased with them. I set out to please him to the best of my ability, and rapidly achieved my aim—that of making him dependent on me. I catered to his every whim. It made me hated in the camp, of course, but I tried to ignore this.

And then, the chance for which I had been waiting came miraculously. Commandant Kistbek was given a promotion! No longer was he the commanding officer of a prison camp in desolate Siberia; he was brought back to civilization and made the head of a Soviet Army post in East Germany.

And I went with him!

It was as I had dreamed from the start. But I had never thought it would come about. Kistbek had been more pleased with me than with any mistress he had ever had. He could not bear to part with me. And so he procured my release, gliding over the fact that I was a dangerous Hungarian rebel, and—as a Soviet officer's mistress—I returned to Europe in style.

I bided my time, living in his household in Germany, submitting with false enthusiasm to his desires. At length he was given leave, and went to East Berlin, taking me along. We caroused all night, drinking champagne smuggled across from the free world. He was drunk; he sang and danced and laughed like a baby, and then he told me to prepare for bed. I was ready for him—with a knife.

His hands groped unsteadily for my breasts; his lips covered mine, his body surged against mine. As he became blindly frenzied with desire, he embraced me, and I jammed the knife deep into his back.

My husband is avenged, I thought.

The rest was simple. I dressed; I woke his chauffeur, who knew and obeyed me. We drove to the border. No one questioned the official car. I crossed safely over into West Berlin. In the morning, I told my story the authorities, and I was flown to West Germany.

I am now living in Western Europe, working quietly for the eventual overthrow of Communism as part of an underground refugee group. Perhaps you may say that it was immoral of me to do what I did, but I answer you that I am more valuable to the cause of freedom where I am now than when I was a prisoner deep in Siberia. And I have taken the life of an enemy of my people. Someday I will have the opportunity for further vengeance on the lust-inflamed butchers who suppressed the liberty of my country and who sated their desires on my unwilling body.

And I have a feeling that the day of my revenge will not be long delayed.

The end

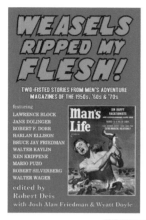

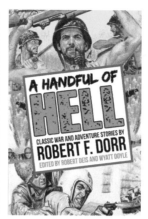

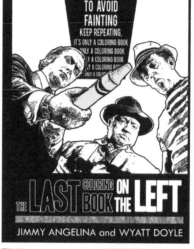

Words and Pictures and Music
Words and Pictures and Music
Words and Pictures and Music

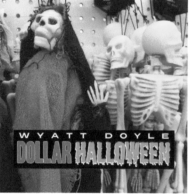

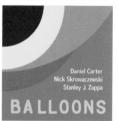

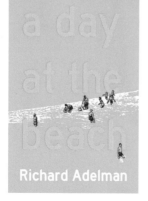
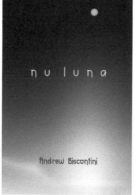

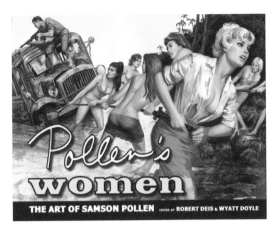

POLLEN'S **women**
THE ART OF SAMSON POLLEN   EDITED BY ROBERT DEIS & WYATT DOYLE

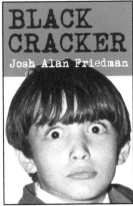

BLACK CRACKER
Josh Alan Friedman

"TELL THE TRUTH
JOSH ALAN FRIEDMAN
UNTIL THEY BLEED"

STOP REQUESTED
WYATT DOYLE
ILLUSTRATIONS BY
STANLEY J. ZAPPA

Words and Pictures and Music

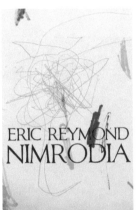

ERIC REYMOND
NIMRODIA

Eric Reymond
*Sub-Sub Librarian,
Extracts on a*

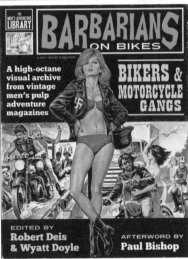

THE MEN'S ADVENTURE LIBRARY

BARBARIANS ON BIKES

A high-octane visual archive from vintage men's pulp adventure magazines

BIKERS & MOTORCYCLE GANGS

EDITED BY
Robert Deis & Wyatt Doyle

AFTERWORD BY
Paul Bishop

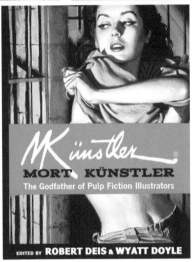

Künstler
MORT KÜNSTLER
The Godfather of Pulp Fiction Illustrators

EDITED BY **ROBERT DEIS & WYATT DOYLE**

Jorge Amaya doesn't live here anymore
PHOTOS BY WYATT DOYLE

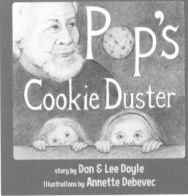

Pop's
Cookie Duster

story by Don & Lee Doyle
Illustrations by Annette Debevec

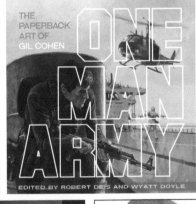

THE PAPERBACK ART OF GIL COHEN

ONE MAN ARMY

EDITED BY ROBERT DEIS AND WYATT DOYLE

The Victorious
Triumph of
Superior
Excellence

STANLEY J. ZAPPA

REV. RAYMOND BRANCH
I'VE GOT HEAVEN ON MY MIND

JIMMY ANGELINA

CAROLINA

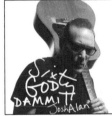

GOD'S DAMMIT
JoshAlan

JON E. EDWARDS
CONTINENTAL INTERNATIONAL

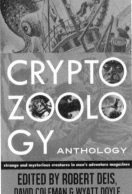

CRYPTO ZOOLO GY
ANTHOLOGY

strange and mysterious creatures in men's adventure magazines

EDITED BY ROBERT DEIS,
DAVID COLEMAN & WYATT DOYLE

THE MEN'S ADVENTURE LIBRARY JOURNAL

I WATCHED THEM
Eat Me Alive

Killer Creatures in Men's Adventure Magazines
EDITED BY ROBERT DEIS & WYATT DOYLE

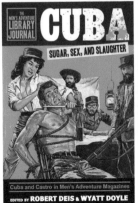

THE MEN'S ADVENTURE LIBRARY JOURNAL

CUBA
SUGAR, SEX, AND SLAUGHTER

Cuba and Castro in Men's Adventure Magazines
EDITED BY ROBERT DEIS & WYATT DOYLE

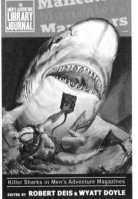

THE MEN'S ADVENTURE LIBRARY JOURNAL

Maneaters
Maneaters
Maneaters

Killer Sharks in Men's Adventure Magazines
EDITED BY ROBERT DEIS & WYATT DOYLE

Words
and
Pictures
and Music

new texture

new texture